bed in a tree

and other amazing hotels from around the world

Bettina Kowalewski

DK

LONDON, NEW YORK, MELBOURNE,
MUNICH AND DELHI

LIST MANAGER Lucinda Smith
SENIOR EDITOR Dora Whitaker
EDITORS Lydia Baillie, Anna Freiberger,
Claire Jones, Juliet Kenny,
Carly Madden, Hugo Wilkinson
EDITORIAL ASSISTANTS Caroline Elliker,
Nicola Malone

TRANSLATORS Christopher Biggs,
Barbara Hopkinson

DESIGN MANAGER Karen Constanti
DESIGNERS Sonal Bhatt, Conrad van Dyk,
Maite Lantaron
SENIOR JACKET DESIGNER Tessa Bindloss
JACKET DESIGNER Meredith Smith
DTP DESIGNER Jamie McNeill

PICTURE RESEARCHER Rhiannon Furbear
CARTOGRAPHERS Casper Morris, Stuart James

PRODUCTION CONTROLLER Rebecca Short

PUBLISHER Douglas Amrine

Reproduced by Media Development Printing
Printed and bound in China by
Leo Paper Products Ltd

First American Edition, 2009
09 10 11 12 11 10 9 8 7 6 5 4 3 2 1

Published in the United States by
DK Publishing, 375 Hudson Street,
New York, New York 10014

www.traveldk.com

Every effort has been made to ensure that this book is as up-to-date as possible at
the time of going to press. Some details, however, such as telephone numbers,
opening hours, prices, and travel information are liable to change. The publishers
cannot accept responsibility for any consequences arising from the use of this book,
nor for any material on third-party websites, and cannot guarantee that any website
address in this book will be a suitable source of travel information. We value the views
and suggestions of our readers very highly. Please write to: Publisher, DK Travel
Guides, Dorling Kindersley, 80 Strand, London, WC2R ORL, Great Britain.

Contents

Foreword   4

① **Ball in a Tree** Vancouver Island, Canada   6

② **In the Doghouse** Idaho, USA   14

③ **Earthships** New Mexico, USA   22

④ **UFO** Mojave Desert, USA   32

⑤ **In a Seashell** Isla Mujeres, Mexico   40

⑥ **Glass Igloos** Lapland, Finland   50

⑦ **Ice Hotel** Norrbotten, Sweden   58

⑧ **Wood Collier's Hut** Västmanland, Sweden   68

⑨ **House on a Lake** Västmanland, Sweden   76

⑩ **Castle** Isle of Mull, Scotland   84

⑪ **Pineapple** Stirlingshire, Scotland   94

⑫ **Gothic Temple** Buckinghamshire, England   102

⑬ **Escape Capsule** The Hague, The Netherlands   112

⑭ **In a Piece of Art** Berlin, Germany   120

⑮ **Inside a Suitcase** Saxony, Germany   130

⑯ **Under the Stars** Westphalia, Germany   138

⑰ **Wine Barrel** Rhine Valley, Germany   146

⑱ **Circus Wagon** Rhône-Alpes, France   154

⑲ **Prison Cell** Lucerne, Switzerland   164

⑳ **Hotel in a Mountain** Ticino, Switzerland   172

㉑ **Cave Hotel** Cappadocia, Turkey   180

㉒ **Bed in a Tree** Sabi Sand Reserve, South Africa   190

㉓ **Elephant Tent** Addo National Park, South Africa   198

㉔ **Glass-Floor Villa** South Ari Atoll, Maldives   206

㉕ **Throat of a Troll** Victoria, Australia   216

㉖ **In a Plane** Waitomo, New Zealand   224

㉗ **Treehouses** Kaikoura, New Zealand   232

Acknowledgments   240

Foreword

IT ALL BEGAN IN AUSTRALIA, when a traveling companion told me of a place in Victoria where you could spend the night inside a troll, entering through its mouth into a subterranean cave-world of stalactites, alcoves, and bedrooms — it sounded absolutely fantastic. What would it be like to spend the night in a place like this? And why in the world would anybody build it? That was it; I was hooked. I began to wonder whether there were other such extraordinary places to stay? That's how the idea was born to make this compilation — a dazzling kaleidoscope of the world's most weird and wonderful hotels.

The selection spans all budgets, from zero- to six-star, and from the most spartan to the ultimate in ostentatious luxury. My only criteria was that it should give you a unique experience, something you just don't come across sitting at your desk in the office, something that will hopefully make you taste a different slice of life.

To complement each hotel experience, I also looked for exciting and unusual things to do nearby. I picked what I thought were the most intense and sensual encounters, be they with culture, history, science, or, above all, with the wonders of nature.... Take a once-in-a-lifetime swim with dolphins, meet elephants and wolves in their natural habitat, fall quiet at the heavenly spectacle of the northern lights, and wander through the surreal moonscapes of Cappadocia — all very powerful experiences you will never forget.

And on another note, I am happy to admit that every hotel surpassed my wildest expectations. There was always far more than I had dared hope — more charming attention to detail, more touching stories, more ever-lasting impressions.... But, don't worry. It wouldn't all fit into this book! Plenty has been left out for you to discover for yourself.

For me, the most surprising discovery had to be the charismatic personalities behind these incredible places to stay — admirable, spirited people brimming with idealism and energy, people who have, against all odds, turned their dreams into reality. Hats off to each and every one of them. Or, perhaps I should better say: hats on and off you go, to discover the world's most amazing hotels!

In the hope of inspiring you to brave a night in a bed with a difference,

Yours,

Bettina Kowalewski

Bettina Kowalewski

PS: If you should come across some amazing place to sleep, or even just hear of one, I'd love to hear all about it, and your suggestions could well end up in another instalment of this compilation! Please drop me a line: **amazinghotels@hotmail.com**

1

VANCOUVER ISLAND
CANADA

BALL IN A TREE

"Suspended in the
air, I can feel the
motion of the
elements – it's as
though I'm
eavesdropping on a
secret conversation
between the trees
and the wind."

IT'S A LONG TIME SINCE OUR EVOLUTIONARY ANCESTORS CAME DOWN FROM THE TREES, but there is still something strangely appealing about the thought of living high up in the treetops, far from the hustle and bustle of life on the ground below.

Here, on wonderful, rugged Vancouver Island in British Columbia, you can do exactly that. Hidden in a small tract of forest near a lake, extraordinary tree dwellings peek out between the leaves. Almost like a pair of gigantic eyes looking around curiously, two huge globes can be seen dangling in the air between the trees.

Each one is suspended in the center of three tall trees by a sturdy network of ropes – and nothing else. No nails have been driven into the wood, nor has any metal or wire touched these trees. Working in harmony with nature is very important to Tom Chudleigh, the creator of the Free Spirit Spheres. He worked on their design and suspension system for five years before he found the perfect balance, which allows them to move ever so gently with the wind.

Together with his charming partner Rosey, this charismatic, bright-eyed man in his mid-50s leads me up a solid spiral staircase into the tree dwelling. My spherical room – named Eryn – is decorated in a rustic yet cozy style: there's a large platform used as a spacious double bed, a dining nook, a galley kitchen, and an additional mezzanine bed. Two large, round windows look out onto the nearby treetops. It feels rather peculiar to be inside a perfect sphere – after all, where else in the world can you experience this? The protective shell surrounding me seems to exude a feeling of security, like an enclosed nest in the trees, or a cocoon.

And this is precisely what Tom has in mind. For him, the Spheres are a place for inner growth and transformation. The spherical shape not only channels and vastly amplifies any sound (just try whispering in the center of the sphere), but also, according to Tom, one's own energy.

The certain "spiritual" element of the Spheres reflects Tom's interest in druid mythology. Even the positioning of the Spheres is significant: the middle of three trees was considered sacred by the druids. And, if you look closely, you can see mysterious shapes carved into the bronze window hinges. These are runes, ancient symbols signifying such things as

TOM CHUDLEIGH (WITH ROSEY COWAN), CREATOR

"To me, the Spheres represent the idea of 'oneness' and unity. There's no separation created by fixed walls as in 'normal' houses, just an inside and an outside. Whenever I have a difficult decision to make, I retreat into the smaller Sphere, Eve, for a while. I find peace there; I tune out all the everyday noise and tune into my 'inspiration channel.'"

"protection, chance to grow" (the rune algiz), "completed life-cycle, harvest" (jera), and "transformation, awakening" (dagaz).

The power of the Spheres seems to have worked once. Having decided to break off her conventional medical treatment in hospital, a young woman, Rosey Cowan, came here as a guest and rented Eve. After two months in her woodland cocoon, she emerged completely transformed. "It was amazing, like a metamorphosis," Tom says. Rosey stayed, and Tom has recently given her Eve as a gift.

It's wonderfully relaxing to lie in bed when all is dark watching the night sky through the round window – which becomes my own kind of oversized eye – and see how the treetops bend and sway gently in the wind. Suspended in the air, I can feel the motion of the elements – it's as though I'm eavesdropping on a secret conversation between the trees and the wind, one that my floating Sphere answers in a gesture of gentle movement.

Free Spirit Spheres
Spiritual cocoon in the trees

● At the time of writing the Spheres were located near Qualicum Beach, Vancouver Island, Canada. However, Tom and Rosey are planning to move to a new location, and when they do both Spheres will move with them. Check website.

ℹ Eve, the smaller Sphere: 9 ft (2.75 m) in diameter, for a single guest or a couple. Eryn: 10.5 ft (3.2 m) in diameter, for up to 3 people. Inside the Spheres: coffee/tea maker, microwave, small fridge. Outhouse in front of the Spheres on the ground. Bathroom, sauna, and kitchen in a separate small building located at the lake around 200 ft (60 m) away. At the time of writing, Tom was working on an additional massage Sphere. Generous snack on arrival; no breakfast. The Spheres can be comfortably heated and are available for rent year-round.

Eve: 100 USD (125 CAD); Eryn: 140 USD (175 CAD). Discount for 2 nights or more.
+1 (0)250 757 9445, cell +1 (0)250 951 9420
www.freespiritspheres.com

Things to do

Fairy-tale forest in Cathedral Grove

This is the perfect day out for those whose night in the treetops has inspired them to delve even deeper into the woods. Not far from the Free Spirit Spheres, Cathedral Grove in MacMillan Park is home to some of the mightiest trees on the island, or even in Canada. The trunk of a Douglas fir can reach up to 9 ft (3 m) in diameter and 30 ft (9 m) in circumference, and the oldest specimens are over 800 years old.

On New Year's Day 1997, a storm ravaged the park felling a number of the ancient and venerable fir trees. Today they lie scattered throughout the woods creating a vast moss-covered landscape that looks like something from a fairy tale. However, their demise has also brought new life to the forest – it has allowed light to penetrate to the forest floor for a new generation of saplings, and has provided many animals with food and shelter. The majestic sight of these mouldering, fallen giants lends the woods a magical, if slightly morbid, atmosphere.

Highway 4 runs more or less straight through the middle of the park, which means it is readily accessible and often very busy. Even so, after only a short distance, you find yourself enveloped by the enchanting woodland scenery. A visit is highly recommended.

Cathedral Grove is around 22 miles (35 km) from the Free Spirit Spheres; take Highway 4 to Port Alberni.

Horne Lake cave tours

Did you know that Vancouver Island has the highest concentration of caves in Canada? Or that it was once covered by a layer of ice 0.6 miles (1 km) thick? As a result of the glacial activity there are over 1,200 caves carved into the island's limestone by the melt water. Seven of these caves are located near Horne Lake and can be explored on guided tours.

The tour is an unforgettable experience – mainly thanks to the enthusiastic tour guides rather than the modest selection of stalactites and stalagmites. On the more demanding tours they lead the group climbing and scrambling through narrow passageways and even across a small underground waterfall. The guides are full of fascinating information on the area's geology and how the cave system was formed. The caves are unlit so helmets with lamps are provided, along with overalls.

Horne Lake is 50 miles (80 km) from the Free Spirit Spheres. Tours range from the 90-min Family Tour (16 USD [20 CAD]) to the Extreme Rappel Tour, which can last up to 5 hrs and costs 125 USD (157 CAD). There are also two caves visitors can explore on their own. Equipment rental only: 6.50 USD (8 CAD).
www.hornelake.com

Kayak trip to the sea lions

Vancouver Island is the largest North American Pacific island. It is about the size of Denmark and has countless smaller islands just off its coast as well as many hidden coves. Exploring the many waterways by canoe or kayak offers some spectacular views and is a popular activity for tourists and locals alike.

A special "female" version of this pastime is available in the small harbor town of Nanaimo. Here, small groups of women gather to explore the many bays by kayak. According to organizer Jan Kretz, these women-only trips usually mean more fun, more camaraderie, and less "Who's going to be first?" During the tours, visitors usually come across violet-colored starfish, curious seals, and sleepy sea lions. On most trips there's also a picnic stop on one of the islands. Jan and her colleagues are friendly, competent kayakers with a great sense of humor. But men, no need to feel left out! Although all-female tours are Jan's specialty, she allows men to join the group on request.

Nanaimo is around 25 miles (40 km) from the Free Spirit Spheres. For beginners as well as experts. Kayaks and equipment are provided. Max 6 participants. Various tours are available. 4-hr Mistaken Island Tour: 48 USD (59.95 CAD).
www.adventuress.ca

Above (left to right): Cathedral Grove; cave near Horne Lake; kayaking past some dozing sea lions

2

IDAHO: USA

IN THE DOGHOUSE

"His muzzle conceals a cozy little platform where kids can cuddle up to sleep or count passing trucks from the windows that are Sweet Willy's eyes."

I'M A B¢B
(208)962-3647

IT IS A KNOWN FACT THAT DOG OWNERS CAN BE OBSESSIVE ABOUT THEIR FOUR-LEGGED FRIENDS: they over-pamper them, worship them – some even go as far as dressing their hair. However, perhaps the ultimate kick for hardcore fans of dogs is spending the night inside one.

In Cottonwood, a small town in Idaho, a large dog stands at a crossroads. Clearly visible from a distance, he is motionless, only his ears flapping now and then. On approaching we soon realize it's an enormous beagle, 33 ft (10 m) high and 17 ft (5 m) wide. This is Sweet Willy, the largest beagle in the world. And tonight we'll end up in his stomach!

Fear not – everything is above board as the tag around Willy's neck proudly proclaims: "I'm a B&B." We soon discover his tummy is the dining room, his rear end the bathroom, and his eyes are the windows.

Sweet Willy isn't alone. He has an older, smaller brother – Toby, a modest 13 ft (4 m) high – standing guard beside him. Next to them a strange scene is played out: a group of men sit happily munching hamburgers at a picnic table, and a bicyclist in a baseball cap is caught in motion crashing into a ditch. It's an exposition of wooden sculpted curiosities in the style of Frances Conklin and Dennis Sullivan, the creators of Sweet Willy. In the store next door are smaller examples of their sculptures to admire and buy. Legions of dogs stand in rank and file: small versions of Sweet Willy beagles, fox terriers, setters, poodles, German shepherds, dachshunds, and golden retrievers – one of which wags his tail. This is Walter, the only real dog at the site, who is lying peacefully in front of Frances and Dennis's workshop. Here they work full-time, seven days a week, at their mutual passion – chainsaw art.

Wanting to inject a bit more fun into his life, Dennis, a former building contractor, taught himself to wield a chainsaw. He met Frances at a dog show in the mid-1980s and persuaded her to follow his lead. Having given up her job as a secretary, she found her new art no more dangerous than using a sewing machine, "You just have to be careful where you put your fingers!" Since then, this likeable, lively team has been creating their pretty wooden sculptures. This is your chance to have your beloved pooch immortalized in wood. Frances and Dennis will gladly carve a replica for you, complete with a golden tag and a red collar, just like Willy's.

When they were starting out Toby, their monumental tribute to chainsaw art, helped bring in the extra business. Strategically placed by the roadside, he's turned the heads of many a motorist and trucker. These giant roadside attractions enjoy a long tradition (by American standards). In the 1940s, as long-distance road travel became popular, enormous three-dimensional advertisements sprang up across America to entice the passing driver. As Toby had proved his talent as an attraction, Dennis and Frances decided to reach for even greater heights. One evening over dinner in Cottonwood's best restaurant they hatched their plan: for the ultimate eye-catcher they would build the biggest dog the world had ever seen. And furthermore – they would let people sleep in it. They were so taken with the idea that Dennis sketched the first draft of Sweet Willy there and then on his napkin.

The perfect spot at a road junction was soon found, and four years later in 2003 Willy welcomed his first guests. Since then, the lives of Dennis and Frances have never been the same. They truly enjoy getting to

Small Dogs
$33
Includes license & training!

FRANCES AND DENNIS, CHAINSAW ARTISTS AND OWNERS

"We don't even consider retirement. Every time a new visitor climbs up the steps to the Dog and opens that door they let out a gasp of wonder and delight. That's what keeps us young. If Sweet Willy manages to put a smile on the faces of passers-by and our guests then that gives us a deep sense of pleasure."

know each and every guest, with or without a dog, and relish the venture as a new enrichment to their lives.

Sweet Willy really is awesome and like nothing you've ever seen before: you reach the front door via the balcony on his belly. His droopy ears are over 12 ft (4 m) long and made from carpet. Inside his belly there is a double bed, a small kitchenette, and a dining area with a view. The furnishings are comfortable and small details have been lovingly added, such as the bedside mutt mat, the dog-shaped bedtime biscuits and even a game of "Dog-opoly." The bathroom is located in his rear. His muzzle conceals a cozy little platform where kids can cuddle up to sleep or count passing trucks from the windows that are Sweet Willy's eyes.

In the evening, just as we're trying to name all the breeds of dog that are carved on the headboard, a strange sound reaches our ears. A scratching, scuffling, scraping noise echoes through the dog house. Is it a tramp looking for a quiet place to sleep? Or

maybe a mouse? We're not really alarmed since, after all, this is a roadside attraction and by definition in constant public view. It's only after looking out from the balcony that we finally realize where the mysterious noise is coming from – it's Willy's ears! As they flap softly in the wind they drag against his wooden body. So we return to our doggy bed and settle down for the night in the world's biggest beagle, a smile on our faces.

Dog Bark Park Inn
Fun and comfortable roadside attraction

 At the crossroads leading into the sleepy village of Cottonwood, Idaho, USA.

Double room in the tummy and a cozy loft for 2 small children in the muzzle. No telephone or TV. Dogs are (who'd have guessed) welcome. Sweet Willy for 2 people: 92 USD; each additional person: 8 USD. Includes a tasty breakfast of Frances's home-made muffins and granola made from handpicked local Idaho fruit. Open Apr–Oct (Sweet Willy hibernates in winter).

+1 208 962 3647
www.dogbarkparkinn.com

Things to do

Appaloosa horse riding
The area around Cottonwood is traditionally the land of the Native American Nez Perce tribe who have lived in this area for thousands of years. Today, they inhabit a reservation close to Lapwai. On Jon Yearout's ranch visitors can ride their famous spotted Appaloosa horses. The horses here are surprisingly friendly, which might be due to Jon's gentle "horse whisperer" way of breaking them in: the horse's will is not broken by force – the animal is patiently driven in a circle until it follows him of its own accord.

Jon is an accomplished guide in this wild and beautiful bear-infested country. To hear more about the history and culture of the Nez Perce tribe you can reserve a Native American guide.

Sweet Water Appaloosa Ranch, Lapwai, is around 40 miles (65 km) from Cottonwood. 2-hr trek for 2 people: 50 USD per person; day trek in small groups (about 5 people): 100 USD per person. Native American guide: 70 USD extra. Rides lasting more than one day are also available.

+1 208 843 2452
www.nezperceappaloosas.net

An encounter with wolves
Meet Sweet Willy's ancestors at The Wolf Education & Research Center in the Nez Perce Reservation. This area was once the natural habitat of the gray wolf (*Canis lupus*), the last wild example of which was shot by a farmer in 1930.

Around a dozen gray wolves, either from private ownership or originally bred for Hollywood film work, spend their autumn years within the fenced area of the Center.

The guides readily share their knowledge of life within the pack and call to attention the wolf's positive role in controlling the population of coyote and other vermin. Half wild and half tame, the wolves are the middlemen between wild prairie beasts and the (often armed) American people. The highlight of the guided tour is, of course, watching the wolves. The best time of day to catch a glimpse of them playing behind the fence is at dusk.

The Wolf Education & Research Center is near Winchester (the town that gave its name to the world-famous Winchester Rifle), around 25 miles (40 km) from Cottonwood. Open Jun–early Sep daily; May and Sep at weekends only; otherwise by arrangement. 2-hr guided tour (max 15 people): 10 USD per person.

+1 888 422 1110 (ext. 3)
www.wolfcenter.org

The Way of the Cross
The Benedictine Monastery of St Gertrude is the major tourist attraction in Cottonwood (besides Sweet Willy, of course). The monastery has around 60 resident nuns who welcome visitors to stay for lunch or, at the very least, a chat.

Behind the monastery a "Way of the Cross" path offers an opportunity for contemplation and prayer. Leading approximately 300 m (980 ft) uphill, it passes a grotto and ends in a peaceful cemetery. There are 14 stops or "stations" along the way depicting the different stages of the Passion of Christ, which invite you to stop for reflection.

If Sister Cecilia has time she'll accompany you along this spiritual path, her remarks and comments finding commendable parallels between the suffering of Jesus and our everyday lives.

The Monastery of St Gertrude (also a historical museum), Cottonwood, is a 10-min drive from Sweet Willy.

+1 208 962 3224
www.stgertrudes.org

Above (left to right): store and workshop at Dog Bark Park Inn; Appaloosa horses; gray wolf in the Nez Perce Reservation; walking the Way of the Cross

3

NEW MEXICO: USA

EARTHSHIPS

"Organically curved walls, green patina light switches, and gorgeous bright stained-glass. The Phoenix suite is like a wondrous showroom for an amazing array of arts and crafts."

EARTHSHIPS

THE AREA AROUND TAOS, NEW MEXICO, is famous for the artists, eccentrics, and visionaries who flock to the high, arid plateau to get in touch with their "inner selves" and live out their dreams. So it's no big surprise that when driving along on the far side of the spectacular Rio Grande Gorge Bridge I spot some strangely futuristic settlements. The buildings are well camouflaged and seem half-submerged in earth mounds that dot the wide plain like molehills. Only the curiously shaped roofs of the buildings rise above the earth, their enormous glass fronts sparkling in the sun. I have arrived at the Earthship World Headquarters.

The Earthships visitor center is located at the front entrance of the extensive sage bush-covered grounds, over which about 60 Earthships are scattered. I almost expect to see Luke Skywalker, or at least a hobbit, step out of the peculiar building. Instead, a young woman with a trendy haircut materializes and gives me directions to the Earthship allocated to me.

As I wind my way through a labyrinth of dusty paths, I'm amazed at the fantastic shapes of the Earthships. No two are alike. Finally I stop in front of an impressive palace-like building. Is this really the right place? It isn't even finished yet! Young men with dreadlocks are pushing wheelbarrows up mounds of soil while a group of women work the cement mixer and others energetically pile up aluminum cans to create a wall. Yes, I am in the right place, this is the Earthship Phoenix. And the fact that my hotel suite is still being built is actually part of the concept: this particular building is also a "show home." The guests who come to stay here are typically of the environmentally and price-conscious type and want to learn how to build Earthships themselves. Earthships are designed to produce their own energy thus rendering them independent of commercial sources, so they are cheap to run as well as resourceful.

The interior of Phoenix seems like a vision from *Ideal Home* magazine. You want plants in your house? An entire jungle of lush (and in part edible!) greenery stretches out along the huge light-flooded glass front of the house. You want space? The enormous living room opens out into the kitchen and on into the bedroom. You like the sound of water? A fishpond with quietly rippling water is being built in front.

MICHAEL REYNOLDS, CREATOR

"In the old days, people looked to the stars to find answers. Today they watch TV. For me, TV raises more questions than answers. I remember watching a documentary in the 1970s that showed how recklessly we were destroying our forests while at the same time mountains of waste were threatening to drown us all. At the time, I was reading about Egyptian priests who would gaze at the night sky from the top of the pyramids. So I did the same: I tied myself on to the roof of my house and looked straight up into the full moon. People thought I was crazy, but I experienced a very powerful vision which has kept me going in my quest to find the best way for us to survive on our threatened planet."

Earthships are typically U-shaped and feature bright, friendly day areas with large glass greenhouse fronts, and dimly lit cozy bedrooms that, since they are hidden beneath the earth, don't have any external windows. No matter where I look, I spy clever decorating touches: organically curved walls, colorful tiles, green patina light switches, and gorgeous bright stained-glass. Ceramic sculptures embellish the kitchen, where cupboard doors have been in-laid with entire branches of trees. The Phoenix suite is like a wondrous showroom for an amazing array of arts and crafts.

During your stay you can watch the creators of these little masterpieces go about their work. The talented team of Earthship builders turns out to be the young "hippies" I met earlier. During the day they sometimes come into my hotel suite to do some more work. While this means you can learn a lot from them firsthand, it does affect your privacy somewhat. A young couple is plastering the chimney in the living room with an imaginative pastel green mural of a troll with a burning fire for a mouth. Tiffany, in her late twenties, is responsible for metalwork. She's sitting on the bare floor, bent over a strip of bronze-colored metal. The ingenious chandelier above the dining table is her creation. It has a delicate wreath of metal leaves and blinks with a thousand small lights. Tiffany first discovered her feel for metal while working in one of the Earthships. Newcomers first try a bit of everything until it becomes clear where they excel. Then, perhaps, they will

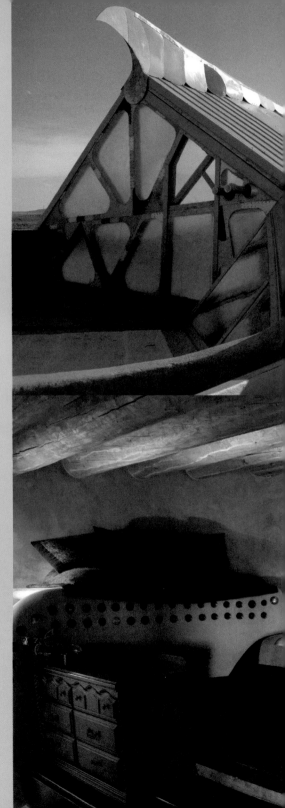

be hired again to apply their talents to a new set of Earthships.

Although the Phoenix is the 60th Earthship built on this patch of land, there is still a certain pioneering spirit in the air, one of achieving a communal goal. The movie *Easy Rider*, which was actually filmed in the area, springs to mind. This is not some kind of whacky cult, however. It's a community with the shared belief in saving the world through the considered use of natural resources.

The clever thing about the Earthships is that they are very energy-efficient and run (almost) off the grid. Solar cells and windmills provide nearly all of the energy needed, and a clever water filtration system re-uses captured rain and snow for drinking, washing, and irrigation. To top it off, Earthships recycle the garbage produced in our affluent society and use it as building material. The thick foundation walls, for instance, have been made from car tires

filled with earth. These were found to be highly effective in retaining heat. The bright dots of color in the bathrooms and even the "flowers" on the walls, on closer inspection, turn out to be the bottoms of glass or plastic bottles. Here, the beauty that lies in the mundane is revealed. But first, of course, someone has had to spot it!

The founder of this idiosyncratic living concept suffered much ridicule early on. Now, with the heightened awareness of climate change, he has become much sought-after as an "eco-guru." Michael Reynolds is an energetic ex-architect in his 60s, his flowing white hair lending him a certain wild dignity. His bright eyes sparkle when we discuss architecture and the future of our planet.

For more than 30 years now, Michael has worked to realize and promote his ideal of sustainable living. Of course, there have been many wrong turns and setbacks along

the way, and changes and improvements are still being made, but Michael's idea has now borne fruit worldwide. Earthships are being built in England, Bolivia, Spain, India, France, Greece, and even in cooler climates such as Scotland.

Anyone interested in new and alternative ways of living will find a stay here a fantastic inspiration. You'll want to grab a shovel and get started right away, building your very own weird and wonderful home. Earthships are houses that are "smart" and in harmony with nature like interestingly shaped arks built to carry us through the difficult times of climate change. A comforting thought that should certainly lead to a good night's sleep....

Earthship World Headquarters
Communal, rustic, inventive

Set in about 1 sq mile (2.6 sq km) of high-desert communal land at an altitude of over 6,500 ft (2,000 m) (you might need a few days to get used to it).

16 miles (26 km) northeast of Taos, 175 miles (280 km) from Albuquerque, New Mexico, USA.

Note that this is not a vacation resort but a communal settlement. New Earthships are constantly being added, and as soon as they are habitable, they are rented out to guests. At the time of writing, the Phoenix was the largest and the most ambitious of the Earthships featuring a large greenhouse with lush "interior jungle", waterfall, and fishpond at the front.

Phoenix studio for 1–2 people including entrance area, bedroom, bathroom, no kitchen: 100 USD; suite for 1–2 people including open fireplace, huge living area with cooking and sleeping area plus additional separate bedroom: 150 USD; suite (as above) for 3–4 people: 225 USD; entire house for 6 people: 275 USD. More intimate and less "grand" are the smaller Earthships: Studio 1 or The Hut.

The community also offers multiple-day Earthship-building workshops.

+1 575 751 0462
www.earthship.org

Things to do

Manby Hot Springs

If you like to experience nature's raw energy, hike down into the nearby Rio Grande Gorge to luxuriate in the bubbling Manby Hot Springs. The 656-ft- (200-m-) high cliff face rising up steeply on both sides of the Rio Grande River provides one of the country's most dramatic backdrops. The springs are heated to a comfortable 100°F (38°C) by volcanic magma, which flows relatively close to the surface here. Ruins of an old bathhouse bear silent witness to the failed attempt by Arthur Manby, a rich Englishman, to build a luxury resort here in the 1920s.

While you are bathing in one of the four thermal springs you can sometimes see bald eagles circling over the gorge. Imposing views into the gorge, cacti, and the scent of sage are your companions along the stony path to the springs.

The Rio Grand Gorge is around 2 miles (3.2 km) or 15 min by car from the Earthships. About 0.3 miles (0.5 km) after the Rio Grande Gorge Bridge turn left on to the unpaved Tune Road. After passing several Earthships, follow the sign to the left to the parking lot. From here the descent to the springs takes about 20 min.

Be a Taos artist for a day

Taos is famous as a center for the arts. One third of its inhabitants are artists, mostly painters. Especially popular are bold colors in the style of Taos' most famous painter, Georgia O'Keeffe (1887–1986). The town is home to around 80 galleries, many of which can arrange individual sessions with artists. Just ask in the gallery of your choice. Sessions must be arranged in advance.

Half-day painting with artists, including painting supplies: around 50 USD. Around half of the galleries belong to the Gallery Association.
www.taosgalleryassoc.com

Taos Pueblo

There's a certain similarity between the Earthships and their precursors in the neighborhood – the adobe houses of the Taos Indians. Built only of earth, water, and straw, Taos Pueblo is thought to be the oldest continuous settlement – nearly 1,000 years – in the US. Today, in a small village of about 50 houses, around 150 Taos Indians, descendents of the Anasazi, live here just as their ancestors did, without electricity or running water. However, many of the buildings are now used for ceremonial purposes only, and their owners live in modern houses nearby. Owners are not permitted to sell their dwellings, and homes are passed down through the generations.

Before the Spanish arrived in the 16th century the buildings had neither windows nor doors and were entered by ladder through an opening in the roof. The pueblo is, even today, seen as a symbol of Indian resistance to exploitation and colonialism. Taos Pueblo is a designated UNESCO World Heritage Site.

Open daily from 8am to 4:30pm in summer; open only by request in winter. Admission: 10 USD, including guide.
+1 575 758 1028
www.taospueblo.com

Above (left to right): paddling in the Manby Hot Springs; cactus plants on the way to the springs; painting the adobe San Francisco de Asis church in Taos; Taos Pueblo

4

MOJAVE DESERT USA

UFO

● UFO

"Fine wires, precisely strung, radiate from the column covering the ceiling in a large spiral pattern similar to a gigantic tesla transformer. It does feel like you're in the midst of a giant physics experiment."

THE MOJAVE DESERT IN SOUTHERN CALIFORNIA is a vast and seemingly empty wilderness. Yet some very strange goings-on have been reported here. Stories of time travel, fountains of youth, and encounters of the Third Kind. Whatever the truth may be, it's definitely worth a closer look!

Driving into the desert from Palm Springs every now and then groups of Joshua trees appear along the roadside, their fantastic gnarled arms raised up into the cloudless sky. Otherwise there's not much else but stones and stillness. And, of course, the baking heat. Finally, a few houses can be picked out in the hilly landscape. This is Landers, a sleepy one-horse town. Further along the very long, very straight road, a white dome can be seen glinting in the distance. Has an alien spaceship landed in the desert? After all, rumor has it the area is pretty popular with visitors from outer space....

On approaching this UFO, I'm first greeted by some very Earthly looking objects. Inside a high perimeter fence there are some picnic tables and slightly worn benches, several hammocks next to a small hut, the odd cactus, and, at the back, a few mobile homes.

Then I see it, bright white against the blue sky, the "UFO" or, more precisely, the Integratron, a domed building 100 ft (13 m) tall with windows all round. There is a curious ring built around it with rods poking out and a metal track running up its side all the way to the roof. It seems someone has put a great deal of thought into the design of this building – but for what purpose exactly?

Joanne Karl, an attractive lady in her early 50s, dressed in flowing wraps, sunglasses, and a cowboy hat, offers some explanation. She is one of three sisters who purchased the Integratron in 2000. Joanne tells me that the building's unique design has mysterious origins. Apparently, it was built following alien instructions!

In the early 1950s – when reports of UFO sightings were two-a-penny in the area – George Van Tassel, an aircraft mechanic and dedicated ufologist, claimed a visitor from the planet Venus had given him instructions for a kind of time machine that would rejuvenate human cells. Acting on these instructions, Van Tassel, with the help of his family, began constructing the thing they called the "Integratron."

Van Tassel combined elements of religious mysticism as well as scientific theory into his design. His influences included the Tabernacle of Moses, the controversial writings of Georges Lakhovsky (1869–1942) on the properties of human cells, and Nikola Tesla's (1856–1943) theories on the wireless transmission of electromagnetic energy. Van Tassel's intent was to "recharge" human cells, a bit like you'd recharge a battery. Interestingly, similar ideas are found in the ancient Chinese concept of Qi as well as in today's space travel research into the effects of ionized radiation on astronauts. Van Tassel spent the rest of his life working to finish the building and activate the Integratron. However, in 1978 he died suddenly (some say under mysterious circumstances) without ever seeing his work in action.

Unfortunately, no-one knows exactly how the wonder machine was meant to work. The only thing that seems certain is that the outer ring was supposed to revolve like a dynamo to generate an enormous voltage of electricity. Van Tassel's plan was to create an incredible 50 megavolts with his machine. To put this in context, a power plant serving a large metropolitan area only produces a voltage of between 220 and 700 *kilo*volts! But, after all, turning back time is no small feat...

JOANNE KARL (MIDDLE WITH HER SISTERS NANCY [RIGHT] AND PATTY), OWNERS

"People have unusual experiences in the Integratron, and a good deal of phenomena take place here. We're in the middle of the desert, yet this building sits at the juncture of three underground rivers. Because of where it is located and the way it is shaped, the building creates some unusual geophysical phenomena that do have an effect on people who come here. I would describe the Integratron as the fusion of art, science, and magic."

The interior of the building is equally unusual: the ground floor is a hall-like room, sparingly furnished with sofas, tables, and piles of plastic chairs. A central wooden column dominates the room. Fine wires, precisely strung, radiate from the column covering the ceiling in a large spiral pattern similar to a gigantic tesla transformer. It does feel like you're in the midst of some giant physics experiment that was never carried out. Today, the workings of this monumental anti-aging apparatus still remain a mystery.

But no reason to despair: Joanne makes up for it in her own way. On the upper floor of the Integratron she focuses on the natural healing and anti-aging powers of body and soul. A wooden dome arches above the spacious open room and on the floor yoga mats with colorful Navajo blankets invite visitors to meditate (remember to take your shoes off!). This "sound chamber," as Joanne calls it, is dedicated to exploring the dome's special acoustics. A stereo system and CDs stand at the ready, and for those who wish to create their own music, or simply make a noise, there are various instruments on hand. There's a didgeridoo, rainsticks, congas, bongos, and an African *djembe*; luckily, there's no need to worry about the neighbors out here in the desert. The seven singing bowls, however, are left for Joanne herself to perform. She gives "sound baths" on request. This is where participants lie on mats, close their eyes, and listen to the soft, almost ethereal sounds of the bowls; they seem to penetrate every fiber of the

body. For Joanne, sound is "nutrition for the nervous system," and she swears by the healing, rejuvenating power of the tones.

The room seems to be a hotbed of spirituality: a small table holds a colorful collection of "holy" objects that have been left behind by visitors to the Integratron. These range from statues of Jesus, Mary, and the angels to Tibetan prayer flags and pictures of the Dalai Lama as well as various feathers and stones. Religious icons mix in with New Age paraphernalia. It's understandable; what place could be better suited to other-worldly communication? The dome of the Integratron seems to act like a gigantic spiritual amplifier, and the legends surrounding its mysterious origin and purpose only serve to reinforce this notion. You can see why, in our rational, de-mythified world, it could be so appealing.

At night, we help ourselves to sleeping bags and yoga mats to make up our beds. It's a bit like camping, which is intentional.

After all, too much comfort might detract from the raw, "otherwordly" effect. We intuitively lie down in the middle of the large room right beneath the dome's center (perhaps so as not to disturb the cosmic order?). I almost jump when a whispered "Good night." seems to be spoken right in my ear so effective are the acoustics in the domed space.

Through the small hole in the middle of the domed roof I can see stars twinkling. They are innumerable out here in the desert, far from the light pollution of any city. The longer I peer up into the sky the more stars appear....

UFO or not, the Integratron was built to benefit humankind, and the people who were involved all wanted to improve the world in some way. With this positive "aura" around us we fall asleep easily. Millions of stars move across the sky above winking at us from their far-off galaxies, be they with or without extraterrestrial life.

Integratron
Other-worldly bonanza for fantasizing physicists

In the Mojave Desert on a back road turning from the small town of Landers. It is 15 miles (25 km) from Joshua Tree, the next town, or 30 miles (45 km) from Palm Springs, California.

First floor: huge round room for meditating and sleeping. It is suggested to bring your own camping mats and sleeping bags although some are available on site. Ground floor: sofas, table and chairs, telescope. No kitchen. The bathroom is in a separate building 100 ft (30 m) away. Outside: hammocks and picnic tables. Especially well suited to groups.

Per person for group bookings: from 40 USD. The Integratron can sleep up to 30 people. 250 USD minimum charge for a night's rental.
+1 760 364 3126
www.integratron.com

Things to do

Climbing in J-Tree
Joshua Tree National Park, or "J-Tree" to those in the know, is a world-famous climbing paradise. Over 400 sites offer 8,000 routes of varying levels of difficulty. The granite rock in the park is nice and rough making it perfect for rock climbing and bouldering. After a stay in the Integratron why not try the climbing route "Rejuvenation" or "Catch A

Falling Star?" There is a great variety of climbs to choose from with alluring names such as "Turtle Soup," "Sexy Grandma," and "Poodles Are People Too" drawing climbers from all around the world to Joshua Tree.

Those needing instruction are well served by Mark Bowling and the team from his climbing school. Mark passes on his knowledge in a calm and reassuring manner. He imparts to the most absolute beginner a new "feeling for stone," leading them up to enjoy breathtaking views over the desert landscape. Shifting your weight, letting go of your grip, and pulling yourself up until you finally reach the summit does give an incredible sense of achievement. It's no wonder that so many get hooked and return to the rocks of Joshua Tree over and over again.

Mark's youngest customer is four years old and his oldest 84. According to Mark the latter now "climbs better than he walks!"

Joshua Tree National Park west entrance, near to where the school meets, is around 20 miles (35 km) from the Integratron. Joshua Tree Rock Climbing School tours: 8am–4pm daily (Jul–Aug: 7am–noon). 1-day course: 125 USD. Equipment, including ropes, harnesses, helmets, and shoes, is provided.
www.rockclimbingschool.com
+1 760 366 4745 or toll-free within the US: 800 890 4745

Desert sculptures
In the middle of the desert, at the end of a dirt road, you can find a special kind of exhibition. What at first appears to be a collection of junk turns out to be just that – junk – but junk assembled to create some extraordinary sculptures.

Mercilessly exposed to the scorching sun, Noah Purifoy's (1917–2004) rusting sculptures have their own unique crude aesthetic, and stand in sharp contrast to the prickly desert flora. Purifoy was an infuential African-American political artist working mainly with "assemblage art." The abstract compositions make use of garbage others have thrown away (old bicycles, bits of scrap metal, hub caps, wooden planks, lavatories, shoes, and trousers, to name just a few) and, standing in the bleak landscape of the desert, offer the contemplative visitor a strange artistic stage from which to ponder themes such as the transitory nature of existence, identity, and tensions between black and white. Materials that seem incompatible are sculpted together, clashing as if in some kind of battle for survival in mute, frozen gestures. The result is sometimes almost tragic, sometimes harmonious, and often quite humorous. This is a very inspiring place. Bring a sun hat!

The Noah Purifoy Outdoor Desert Art Museum of Assemblage Sculpture, Joshua Tree, is around 9 miles (14 km) from the Integratron. Free (although more formal paying tours are planned). No restrooms.
+1 213 382 7516
www.noahpurifoy.com

Exploring Joshua Tree National Park
Covering over 1,200 sq miles (3,000 sq km), Joshua Tree National Park is, unsurprisingly, home to the distinctive knobbly Joshua tree (*Yucca brevifolia*). These oddly shaped trees lend the desert landscape an otherworldly charm.

In fact, Joshua trees aren't really trees, nor are they cacti as one might assume. They're actually a type of large lily, also known as the Giant Yucca. The largest grow to 49 ft (15 m) tall, with the oldest reaching an astonishing 900 years of age. Joshua trees only grow in the southwest USA mostly within the Mojave Desert in the northwest side of Joshua Tree Park. This area lies between 3,300 and 6,600 ft (1,000–2,000 m) above sea level and, for a desert, is relatively cool and damp. The Joshua trees don't grow in the Colorado Desert in the eastern part of the park, which is hotter and at a lower altitude.

Park Rangers offer free scheduled tours, and it is fascinating to learn about the animals and plants that have adapted to the extreme conditions here. In order to avoid undue loss of moisture in their leaves, many desert plants carry out photosynthesis in their stems. The dry shrubs that look vaguely familiar are actually a desert variety of the oak tree, but with tiny leaves!

For those who want to set out on their own but learn something along the way, the park also offers 12 short, self-guided nature trails with information panels. Each of the trails has its own special features. Particularly popular is "Hidden Valley," which is a 1-mile (1.5-km) loop dotted with huge, picturesque boulders. There is also "Cottonwood Spring," which has a shady palm tree oasis, and the "Barker Dam" trail, where you might be lucky enough to spot a desert Bighorn Sheep, the largest animal in the park.

The park's west entrance is around 20 miles (35 km) from the Integratron. Free Ranger Tours run from Oct–May. Tours are for 1–3 hrs. Bring at least a gallon (4 liters) of water per person, per day. Park entrance fee: 15 USD per car, valid for one week.
www.nps.gov/jotr

Above (left to right): scaling a cliff face in Joshua Tree National Park; desert sculpture *From the Little People's Point of View* (1994) by Noah Purifoy; Joshua Tree National Park

5

ISLA MUJERES: MEXICO

IN A
SEASHELL

"There are two
seashell houses: one
tall, upright shell in
the form of a conch
and a round, squat
one sitting next to it
– architectural
masterpieces
inspired by the
original designs of
Mother Nature."

ISLA MUJERES IS A SMALL CARIBBEAN ISLAND, surrounded by white sandy beaches and a turquoise ocean, 9 miles (14 km) off the coast of Cancún, Mexico. The north of the island, where the ferries dock, throngs with bustling tourists and colorful souvenir stores while the south is quiet and peaceful. Here, the golf cart-driving tourists stop to take a picture of one famous island curiosity – a giant habitable seashell!

In fact, there are two seashell houses, shining so white they nearly hurt your eyes: one tall, upright shell in the form of a conch and a round, squat one sitting next to it – architectural masterpieces inspired by the original designs of Mother Nature. And what could be more fitting on an island whose beaches (especially in the south) are covered with giant seashells?

In the 1990s architect Eduardo Ocampo arrived on the island and built an attractive little house for himself and his wife, Raquel. He didn't stop there, however. To make sure his beloved brother Octavio would come and visit as often as possible, Eduardo decided to build him a house, too, right in the garden. Of course, this couldn't possibly be any old house. Octavio is a famous painter and would need something suitably creative. Eduardo walked down to the beach to think it over ... When he pulled a large queen conch from a pile of shells, he had his answer. This was exactly what his brother's house would look like: jagged on the outside, rounded on the inside; the staircase in the form of a spiral, just like the inside of the shell; a door where the shell's mouth would be and windows shaped like the holes in an old shell.

It was the perfect design for Octavio, whose "metamorphic" paintings are renowned for their optical illusions (his portraits, on closer inspection, turn out to be composed of birds and twisted branches, for example, his landscapes of women's bodies). And, sure enough, Octavio was thrilled with his new island abode. In fact, so much so that he wanted a second one built for all the friends he always brought along! This time a round shell served as the model. Eduardo glued the two inspirational seashells onto a piece of wood and used this as the template for his giant seashell houses. Even today the model is part of the décor and can be found in the larger seashell's living room.

The brothers designed the interiors of the houses together. Painted in a rather stark seashell-white, the décor is not particularly lavish or plush. However, what it may lack in luxury it more than makes up for in originality: in the bathroom water flows from real seashell "faucets" into a sink made from a giant clam shell. There's a small palm tree in the living room and on the balcony a bleached tree trunk serves as a railing. Eduardo found all these natural treasures on the local beach and incorporated them into the seashell houses with his own fair hands. The rooms are further decorated with a multitude of seashells, ornamental black sea fan coral, and, on the wall, two of Octavio's maritime-themed paintings in his "metamorphic" style. Since Octavio has become so busy as an artist – with customers including Jane Fonda and Cher – he is now only able to stay at the seashell houses for a few weeks each year. The rest of the time these exceptional lodgings are available to rent.

The Caribbean air is humid, salty, and hot. Paint peels off so quickly here that the seashell houses have to be repainted every six months. In the stifling heat, the view from the balcony reveals a refreshingly cool play of colors: the white of the seashells meets the blue of the sky where every now

EDUARDO OCAMPO (WITH RAQUEL AQUILAR), BUILDER AND MANAGER

"I wanted to build something special for Octavio and, in the end, nature provided the model. It was my goal to create a really natural, rustic house, making use, as much as possible, of things that had been washed up on the beach. I love using natural materials in my buildings and I was delighted to be able to do this here to such a great extent."

and then a gray pelican soars by majestically, or a black frigate bird drifts into view, suspended seemingly motionless in the air. Below, the swimming pool glitters a deep blue in contrast with the bright turquoise of the ocean beyond. And, in the distance, the shimmering beach can be seen carpeted with sun-bleached shells of many forms and kinds — some of them small and round, others tall and jagged.

Casa Caracol
Rustic-maritime

Located on the quiet south end of Isla Mujeres, which is readily accessible and developed for tourists. The sea is about 160 ft (50 m) from the seashell houses across a road while access to the beach is about 0.5 miles (1 km) away. Not far from here part of the Mesoamerican Reef, the second largest coral reef in the world, stretches along the Mexican coast.

Tall, upright seashell: double room, modern open kitchen, living room, two bathrooms, air-conditioning. Not suitable for young children due to unsecured balconies. Small, round seashell: double room, bathroom. Pool. From 1,500 to 1,960 USD (20,000 to 26,000 MXN) per week.
+1 773 640 4906
www.mayaneyes.com

Things to do

Beach life
Don't miss the chance to go snorkeling off the beach of Hotel Garrafón, five minutes by golf cart from the seashell houses. Here, the fish are so tame you might well find yourself swimming in a cloud of them swarming all around you — an unforgettable experience. This is also a great place to watch pelicans come in for a clumsy landing on wooden posts in the water.

Isla Contoy – the island of birds
Isla Contoy, a tiny jewel for nature lovers, especially bird lovers, lies approximately 45 minutes by boat from Isla Mujeres. The island is a nature reserve and is completely uninhabited except, that is, for about 150 different types of sea birds who frequent the island. Half of these are migratory birds from South and Central America and Alaska. In the middle of the island is a mangrove lagoon where you can usually find nesting frigate birds.

With a massive wingspan of up to 8 ft (2.4 m), the huge birds are fascinating to watch as they feed their chicks or take to the air. With any luck, you'll also be able to spot a crocodile or a dogfish since both raise their young in this protected section of water. Horseshoe crabs, known as "living fossils," can also be seen walking around on the sea bottom (they can't swim). An information center on the island offers guided tours (in Spanish only). There is also a self-guided nature trail with signs providing information (in English) about the island's flora and fauna. If you hear a strange thud while exploring the trail, don't be afraid, it's just an iguana falling from a tree.

As well as these natural highlights, the long, thin Isla Contoy offers all the pleasures of a quintessential, picture-postcard Caribbean island. It has palm-fringed, white

beaches and a turquoise lagoon where a friendly stingray often makes a visit ... much to the delight of bathers. Visitor numbers to the island are limited; the fishing co-operative and two private tour operators depart from Isla Mujeres and larger boats come from Playa del Carmen.

Isla Mujeres Fishing Co-op has a booth in the Av Rueda Medina. Day trip including a delicious lunch (fresh fish) and time to spend on the beach: 70 USD (920 MXN).
+52 998 877 1363
www.islacontoy.org

Exploring underwater caves

Along the Mayan Riviera south of Cancún you can find the Yucatán's well-hidden but truly spectacular attraction – the cenotes. These are subterranean caves filled with crystal-clear fresh water that provide divers with a magical underwater world to explore. The Yucatán is made up of limestone and contains a huge system of underground rivers and caves, the largest on Earth according to the latest research. A cenote is a sinkhole that forms when the rock ceiling of a cave collapses and creates a point of access to the underground cave world. The ancient Maya spun many myths around the cenotes, and used them for religious ceremonies as well as a source of precious fresh water.

In shallow waters often up to 50 ft (15 m) deep, divers can carefully swim between stalactites and stalagmites, admire cathedral-like underwater halls, and search for fossils – or even human bones (the remains of sacrifices). Visibility is excellent; on sunny days, rays of light create an enchanting "laser show" in the water. Each cenote has its own special feature and character: some are known for their light effects, others for their plant life, bat caves, or even clouds of sulfur. However, simply swimming and snorkeling in a cenote – often hidden in

the midst of lush vegetation – is a wonderfully refreshing treat. To get a deeper look at the underground caverns you will need a diving certificate for open water, and, for greater depths with no natural light, a special certificate for cave diving. Diving is only permitted with a guide.

Recommended cenotes include Tankah for swimming; Azul for young children since it features warm pools; Dos Ojos for excellent stalactite and stalagmite formations; Taj-Mahal for its fossils; Ponderosa for its aquatic plants; and Chac Mool for its especially pretty light displays.

Privately owned cenotes often have low entrance fees of around 4 USD (50 MXN) including snorkel rental. There are many organized diving tours available. Most offer two dives for around 80 USD (1,100 MXN). Ask at the tourist office on Isla Mujeres.
+52 998 877 0307 (tourist office)

Mayan ruins of Tulúm

As the only ruined Mayan city located directly on the Caribbean coast, Tulúm is one of the country's most popular tourist attractions. It's not hard to see why – the ancient gray monuments are dramatically positioned on a 40-ft- (12-m-) high cliff overlooking the ocean, their backdrop the turquoise water and the sparkling white beaches of the Caribbean. It's an enthralling combination of historical mystery and exotic scenery.

In its heyday around AD 1250–1500 (the Late Post-Classic period) the temple complex was a Mayan religious center. Probably the only people allowed to live within its 20-ft- (6-m-) thick walls were members of the ruling class and the highest-ranking priests. The Maya lived according to five different calendars: celestial, solar, lunar, ceremonial, and mathematical. Throughout religious ceremonies, which could last up to five days, fasting was strictly observed. According to Mayan beliefs, there were 9 hells and (thankfully) 14 heavens.

Experienced guides, who are available for rent at the entrance, can provide many more interesting facts. It's worth the extra expense because the guides really bring the fascinating stories of Mayan culture to life.

Wooden stairs lead down to the beach. Unfortunately, although many do, swimming against the spectacular backdrop of the Tulúm ruins is not safe due to strong undercurrents.

From Isla Mujeres: 30 min by ferry to Cancún, then 80 miles (130 km) via highway to Tulúm. The entrance is extremely touristy and has countless souvenir stores. Open May–Oct: 8am–7pm; Nov–Apr: 7am–6pm. Admission: 4 USD (48 MXN). Tulúm by Night tour: 8–10pm; 22 USD (290 MXN). Guide for up to 6 people (highly recommended): around 30 USD (400 MXN).

Above (left to right): harbor of Isla Contoy; swimming and snorkeling in a cenote; beach beside the Mayan city of Tulúm

6

LAPLAND. FINLAND

GLASS IGLOOS

GLASS IGLOOS

"As though choreographed by a cosmic director, shimmering curtains of green, yellow, and violet undulate in a magical dance across the heavens. It is a breathtaking, unforgettable spectacle of nature."

IN FINLAND, WHEN THE FIRST SNOW FALLS, it's a tradition that parents build an igloo for their children. So it was in the Eiramo family, to the great delight of young Jussi. He was so enchanted that he didn't want to leave his igloo and even begged his parents to stay the night, but to no avail. One fine winter, 20 years later, Jussi was finally able to realize his childhood dream. He built a handful of igloos out of snow to offer what was possibly the first ever vacation resort with igloo accommodations. However, he soon came up with an even more ingenious plan.

Today, looking just like neatly landed spaceships, 20 glass igloos are lined up in three rows at the edge of some woods above a river. Double layers of thermal-paned glass ensure that the domes' windows do not ice up. In fact, it's the same special glass that is used on icebreakers at sea whose windows can never be allowed to freeze over. Even when storms rage outside and the temperature sinks below -22°F (-30°C), as is often the case here, it remains cozy and warm inside the igloos.

In my plain yet functionally furnished igloo, not only the glass walls but also the floor is heated. A waist-high curtain hangs around the room, scarcely protecting the two plush, electronically adjustable beds from prying eyes – the darkness must do the rest. Once I've snuggled up in bed I hardly dare close my eyes in case the sky becomes filled with color, and the dazzling spectacle of the northern lights – the *aurora borealis* – begins. Then, as though choreographed by a cosmic director, shimmering curtains of green, yellow, and violet undulate in a magical dance across the heavens. It is a breathtaking, unforgettable spectacle of nature.

Kakslauttanen is one of the best places on the planet to observe the northern lights, a play of light that lasts anywhere from three minutes to several hours. At this latitude it occurs at least every other night between September and April. However, the skies must be clear and you must be awake. The northern lights are a natural phenomenon that were scientifically explained only in the 1960s. The effect is produced when charged particles brought by the solar wind discharge their energy at a height of about 90 miles (150 km) in the Earth's atmosphere.

In the far north of Scandinavia every season has its special appeal. My absolute favorite is fall, when, from the middle of

JUSSI EIRAMO, OWNER

"I began my career panning for gold up on the river as many others do here. Soon I was able to open my first sauna with a little café and eight rental cabins on the side. Then finally, I built my snow igloos. The guests loved them. But then I saw them going outside at night to watch the northern lights and they were all shivering with cold. Well, that was no good! I thought it over and finally hit upon the idea: igloos, heated and made of glass!"

September, the leaves turn and the wide plains of Lapland light up in intense colors — a phenomenon known as "Ruska." The northern lights can be clearly seen and the air is wonderful — clear, marvelously fresh, and smelling of pine. This is the time to go out and gather berries, especially lingonberries and cranberries, and then a little later much sought-after mushrooms such as boletes, milk caps, and porcini.

It is peaceful here and utterly still. Squirrels chase each other outside the front door of my igloo. There are also foxes, even eagles, a few shy bears, and last, but certainly not least, great numbers of reindeer. In this part of the world there are roughly eight times as many reindeer as people; Kakslauttanen is actually an old word meaning "reindeer meat cache." You'll see fewer of the free-running reindeer in the fall, however, since the indigenous Sami people herd them together with their calves before the first snowfall in October.

Below the igloos, a clear river feeds into a small lake where salmon fishing is permitted every three years (ask Jussi if you are interested). Its water is so pure that you can drink from it. In fact, the hotel's tap water is drawn from the nearby rivers, which harbor many springs.

After spending the night in a glass igloo, guests can enjoy a traditional Finnish sauna — a smoke sauna, which is actually the original of all saunas. Unlike modern, electrically heated saunas, a smoke sauna is heated laboriously with burning logs. According to Jussi, the one here in Kakslauttanen is the largest in the world.

The hotel grounds are extensive. As you walk through them to the hotel restaurant for breakfast and dinner (reindeer steak is, of course, on the menu!) you come across interesting, often very humorous, sculptures dotted here and there across the landscape. Every year Jussi commissions a European artist to create a sculpture that captures the unique quality of Kakslauttanen. I know what this would be for me; it would be the close proximity to the Lapland wilderness and its stunning natural phenomena, most intensely experienced when you lie down in bed at night, not surrounded by walls, but beneath a transparent glass skin!

Igloo Village Kakslauttanen
Close to nature. Wilderness adventure

Kakslauttanen, Finland. 4 miles (6 km) south of Saariselka, 25 miles (40 km) south of Ivalo (Finland's northernmost airport).

Twenty glass igloos, each with sink and toilet, are arranged in three rows. The front row offers the best views, some of the river. Also on offer are log cabins, 20 snow igloos, and a traditional Finnish peat house. A large thermal-paned glass tepee is available to all guests for relaxing and socializing in the evenings.

Glass igloo including breakfast, dinner and morning sauna: one person 275 USD (210 EUR); two people 350 USD (266 EUR). Closed Jun–late Aug.

+358 (0)16 667 100
www.kakslauttanen.fi

Things to do

Hiking and berry picking in the National Park

Lapland's fantastic wilderness and wide-open spaces are best experienced in summer or fall by hiking through the Urho Kekkonen National Park, Finland's second largest national park. Choose your tour route from an extensive network of trails ranging from a 1-mile (2-km) circular trail to one taking several days.

Those wishing to explore the unique flora and fauna that exist beyond the Arctic Circle can walk with a guide such as Reima Mustonen. Reima feeds his group with interesting facts (did you know, for instance, that in winter reindeer graze on a white lichen that only grows in places where the air is pure?) and in season, he'll take you to the tastiest berries and mushrooms. In July, for example, he'll lead you to the prized cloudberry (*Rubus chamaemorus*), which contains 20 times more vitamin C than an orange.

Once back in Kakslauttanen, you can help the cook prepare traditional recipes using the manifold treasures you gathered along the way.

Reima picks up the tour group in Kakslauttanen. He speaks English, German, and Swedish and always seems to have just the right dictionary with him. 3-hr guided walk: up to 4 people 105 USD (80 EUR) per person; 5 or more people 130 USD (100 EUR) per person.

+358 (0)40 541 0240, cell +358 (0)16 350 176
www.saariselka.fi

Trout fishing in Lake Inari

Lake Inari, the largest lake in Lapland with its 3,300 islands, is famous for its abundance of trout. It is, beyond any doubt, an angler's paradise. Going on a fishing trip by boat with Erkki Halmetoja is a great experience for beginners and seasoned anglers alike. Erkki is the proud owner of a mountain ("a man needs his mountain"), which offers a beautiful view of the lake.

Before embarking on the excursion he more than gladly demonstrates the traditional method for making tar, the staff of Finnish life that locals honor in their saying, "When vodka, sauna, and tar no longer help, then it's way too late."

Then we set off. On board the boat, six rods are mounted to attract the trout during the leisurely voyage. Erkki shows us how to use the equipment and lets everyone have a try. There are seven different kinds of trout in Lake Inari, among them the salmon trout and the Arctic char, which is only found in very cold waters. We land on beautiful Jääsaari Island (Ice Island) to grill the fish we have caught over an open fire. If no-one has had any luck (as can happen sometimes when the north wind is too strong), Erkki prepares a meal with his own back-up supplies!

Meet Erkki at Ivalo, about 25 miles (40 km) from Kakslauttanen. From here he takes you to his mountain 6 miles (10 km) away before continuing on to nearby Lake Inari. 6–7-hr trip: for 1–2 people 180 USD (135 EUR) per person; 3 or more people 145 USD (110 EUR) per person. Includes lunch on the island. Equipment is provided.
+358 (0)16 667 260
www.ivaloadventures.fi

Pan for your own gold

The gold rush was not unique to California. Lapland, too, had a gold rush that began in 1868 when gold was discovered in the Ivalo riverbed close to Kakslauttanen. This is where Jussi began his career. Today, around 50 professional golddiggers still make their living searching for gold. One of them is Paavo Holmisto, a jovial man in a cowboy hat and checkered shirt, who now spends a large part of his time helping tourists find their own piece of gold.

After a short introduction to the history of the Lapland gold rush, would-be golddiggers sit on the edge of a pool and sift and wash, and sift and wash their pans under Paavo's tutelage. Then, with fingers that seem way too thick and clumsy for the job, miniscule kernels of gold dust are picked out. This method works only because gold is 18 times heavier than ordinary sand. But be careful! Don't agitate or tip the pan too vigorously or everything will land back in the pool, including those glittering objects of desire you have been working so hard to find. Everyone on this excursion should be able to find a teensy bit of gold to take home – your very own self-panned gold!

Guests are picked up from Kakslauttanen. 4-hr "Nature, Golddigging, and Culture": 90 USD (69 EUR). Includes a short hike of about 1 mile (2 km) to the riverbed. Rubber boots are provided.
+358 (0)16 668 706
www.saariselka.fi/luontoloma

Above (left to right): wooden sculpture in the grounds of the Igloo Village, Kakslauttanen; lingonberries ripening; fishing on Lake Inari; panning for gold near the Ivalo riverbed

7

NORRBOTTEN:
SWEDEN

ICE HOTEL

ICE HOTEL

"Once inside the
hotel, I begin to feel
a strange new
affinity with the ice.
The beautifully
sculpted figures
entice me to run my
fingers along them."

A HOTEL BUILT FROM SCRATCH EVERY YEAR ANEW, the Icehotel is a dream in ice and snow come true.

One hundred and twenty-five miles (200 km) north of the Arctic Circle, in deepest Lapland, where the northern lights shine, lies the peaceful little village of Jukkasjärvi. There is a small supermarket, a cozy restaurant, a souvenir store, and Sweden's oldest wooden church. Other than that there are only the dogs, sled dogs that is, more of them than inhabitants in fact ... and the wintry expanse of the great white open.

On the banks of the frozen River Torne, which here widens out to a lake, stands the region's main tourist attraction: the Icehotel – the first, the original, the mother of all ice hotels.

The idea was born in 1990 during an exhibition of ice sculptures when, due to a shortage of hotel rooms, a group of visitors armed with reindeer hides and sleeping bags decided to sleep in the "Arctic Hall" – a structure that had been built from ice blocks specially for the exhibition. The next morning the intrepid guests were ecstatic about their icy night's experience. And so, the plans for the first ever ice hotel were conceived. It has been re-built every year since then.

With an area of approximately 16,400 sq ft (5,000 sq m), it's the world's biggest ice hotel, complete with an ice reception desk, a colonnaded ice hall, numerous ice sculptures, and, in all, 64 icy rooms and suites. There is also an ice chapel, where Sunday services and weddings are held, an ice bar with a live video link to its twin – the Icebar in Stockholm, and an ice theater, in which Shakespeare, and only Shakespeare, is regularly performed.

In late fall, when the wild River Torne freezes over, huge blocks of crystal-clear ice are hewn from its turquoise depths. Every year, a fresh group of artists designs and builds the new hotel, which means that every year the hotel is different and unique.

Once inside the hotel, I begin to feel a strange new affinity with the ice. The beautifully sculpted figures entice me to run my fingers along them. Their cold but surprisingly smooth surfaces feel soft to the touch. Everything around me is made of ice: the walls, the floors, the light fittings, and even the furniture – tables, chairs, and, yes, even the beds! In fact, even the elegant glasses in the Icebar are made from the

ARNE BERGH, ARTISTIC DIRECTOR

"Each year we invite between 30 and 40 artists from around the world to join us in building the Icehotel. Not only sculptors, but all kinds of innovative people are involved, from architects to fashion and web designers. Each November, we collaborate for two weeks on the design of the new hotel. These are always the two most creative and intense weeks of the year."

clear ice of the river, its waters so pure that the local people drink from it in the summer.

To make my stay as comfortable as possible, the Icehotel supplies me with warm clothing: a very hip-looking fur hat, ski overalls, waterproof boots, and, for this special night, a thick Arctic sleeping bag. In the evening, the constant flow of day-trippers slowly ebbs away until the Icehotel, in all its illuminated glory, falls at last into the possession of those who are staying the night.

On entering my icy suite I'm reminded of a camping adventure. There's no door, because the frame is slowly but surely melting away; only a felt curtain separates my bedroom from the hallway. The temperature in Celsius is five degrees — below zero that is. I quickly get into my cozy sleeping bag and discover gratefully

that I have not been put straight on ice. There's a thick mattress topped with a reindeer hide between me and the cold stuff, hide being one of the most effective types of insulation Mother Nature has to offer. Nevertheless, it's reassuring to know that the hotel's hot and steamy sauna awaits me in the morning.

It's fascinating to think that just a few months ago, a shoal of salmon may have swum through the waters that now make up my bed. I can even see small bits of vegetation that have been trapped in the clear ice, like strange creatures from another age caught and preserved in turquoise-colored resin. But it's not forever. Only until spring, when this majestic palace in all its splendor begins to melt, returning what it has borrowed back to the mighty River Torne.

Icehotel
Peaceful, artistic, cool

 Jukkasjärvi, Lapland, Sweden.

Price for 2 people including breakfast, sauna, and warm clothing: undecorated "Snow room" 460 USD (3,800 SEK); "Ice room" suite with ice sculptures (highly recommended) 590 USD (4,900 SEK); luxury "Art suite" 700 USD (5,800 SEK); "warm" rooms in wooden chalets and bungalows 410 USD (3,390 SEK). Open mid-Dec–late Apr (depending on the winter).
+46 (0)980 66800
www.icehotel.com

Things to do

Dog sledding
Simply a must when in Jukkasjärvi. It feels like a dream, racing through a winter wonderland, no sound but the swish of the sled and the panting of the dogs, chasing over frozen lakes and through snow-powdered forests. Rides include a campfire coffee break with the sled dogs howling in the background.
   1.5-hr trip: 190 USD (1,595 SEK); 4-hr trip with lunch: 355 USD (2,950 SEK).
Reserve via Icehotel

Ice sculpting course
For budding artists, the Icehotel offers a unique chance for a hands-on experience working with ice as an artistic medium. The ice proves to be a surprisingly soft medium to work with as you create your own ice sculpture under expert supervision. Sadly, you won't, for obvious reasons, be able to take your masterpiece home with you!
   2-hr ice sculpting course: 70 USD (595 SEK).
Reserve via Icehotel

Reindeer sleigh ride and Sami culture
Take a ride on a real sleigh and find out why Santa still prefers sleighs to more modern forms of transportation. With the help of an indigenous Sami guide dressed in traditional brightly colored costume, you can have a try at driving a reindeer sleigh through the snow. The excursion also includes a short ride on a snow-mobile to feed the reindeer herd, and the chance to try traditional Sami food, including reindeer meat roasted over an open fire in the Lavvu (a Sami tent). The guide tells stories about the history and culture of the Sami people while you enjoy the food.
   3.5-hr experience: 200 USD (1650 SEK).
Reserve via Icehotel

Above (left to right): dog sledding; harnessed sled dog; ice figure in the hotel; learning how to sculpt with ice; reindeer

8

VÄSTMANLAND:
SWEDEN

WOOD COLLIER'S HUT

WOOD
'COLLIER'S
HUT

"The men cut the
wood and pile it up
to be used on the
fire. The air is filled
with the smell of
pine and fragrant
smoke from the fire."

WHOEVER COMES TO KOLARBYN, Sweden, might think they have arrived in the land of trolls. Pine trees as far as the eye can see are interspersed with boulders, and in the distance a lake shimmers. Among the trees huddle a dozen large mounds, overgrown with foliage.

What might initially look like grassy hillocks are, in fact, huts, complete with a door and a small chimney protruding from the roof. Beside each hut is a metal bucket and a large pile of what seems to be coal slack. And that's exactly what it is. Kolarbyn is a settlement of 12 authentic wood collier's huts, scattered in the dappled sunlight of the forest amid a sea of billberries. Shelters such as these have existed since the 17th century when charcoal was produced by burning large amounts of wood built into a mound in the forest. It was still a common practice in Kolarbyn until the 1960s.

As industrialization progressed, the wood collier's trade slowly began to disappear. In acknowledgment of the tradition and in an attempt to pass it on to future generations, colliers from the nearby village of Skinnskatteberg built these huts in 1996. Unfortunately, they were not maintained and became somewhat dilapidated. Then, in 2003, a young fellow arrived on the scene looking for a place to accommodate the guests of his moose safaris. He fell in love with the idyllic, remote location and decided to open a youth hostel in spite of, or even because of, its extreme intimacy with nature.

The lack of electricity at Kolarbyn alone constitutes quite an adventure for most of us. In the pitch black of the windowless huts the only source of light comes from a few candles and an old-fashioned, but here rather useful, gas lamp. Of course, there's no stove. Meals and morning coffee are prepared around the camp fire giving everyone a perfect opportunity to socialize. The men cut the wood and pile it up to be used on the fire. The air is filled with the smell of pine and fragrant smoke from the fire. Kolarbyn seems to be especially popular with bicyclists and is also a true paradise for families. Kids can roam around freely – running down to the lake for a swim or collecting bilberries in the woods.

Simple modern conveniences we take for granted do not exist in the middle of the forest. There is no running water. Drinking water is supplied in large drums, and when children arrive at the hostel everyone

MARCUS JONSON, HOSTELIER

"When the committee from the Youth Hostel Association arrived, the gentlemen in suits said, 'Yes, very nice, but where's the hostel?' It was really quite funny. Many of the expected standards simply didn't apply at Kolarbyn. Like the childproof light sockets, for example, or the obligatory window blinds – well, we don't have electricity here, or even windows!"

ventures out with Marcus to replenish the drums with fresh water from the spring. On the way he tells the children about the magical qualities of the spring water the first sip of which grants the drinker a wish! But, as Marcus explains, the wish will only come true for those who can make it to the spring perfectly quietly and without talking – a condition that has varying degrees of success!

Of course, don't forget that the lack of running water also means outhouse toilets, but Marcus has managed to give even these a nostalgic touch with candlelight, water bowl, and an enamel jug. Kolarbyn is an eco-lodge and garbage is either collected and separated or, if appropriate, burned on the fire.

Twice a year a traditional charcoal burning takes place, and young and old from the surrounding villages come to Kolarbyn to learn the process. Everyone joins in as the local colliers build up a large pile of wood 5 ft (1.5 m) high, which is then sealed with twigs to keep out the oxygen. The pile is lit and the process of turning wood into charcoal begins. Every two hours somebody has to attend to the smouldering pile, even throughout the night. The complete process takes about ten days, and when the pile has finally burned out the result is a great heap of home-made charcoal. The coal is divided up between everyone who helped, and the remainder is sold to raise money for the upkeep of Kolarbyn.

If you are planning to visit Kolarbyn, you might want to come prepared: a simple flashlight may not be in keeping with Marcus's purist style but will prove invaluable at night. Those who suffer from back problems should be aware that only a camping mat is supplied to cushion the hard wooden bunks.

Kolarbyn is a place for hardcore nature lovers – and is probably the most extreme youth hostel in the world.

Kolarbyn
Nature extreme! Informal and sociable

◉ Located in the middle of the forest near Lake Skärsjön, Västmanland, Sweden. The closest village with a supermarket is Skinnskatteberg, 2 miles (3 km) away.

ℹ Youth hostel without electricity or running water, but with a campfire, candles, and a freshwater spring. Windowless huts with open fireplace and two bunks; a basic third bed can be fitted. Sleeping bags are available to rent. Bilberry season from the end of July until September followed by wild mushroom season (chanterelles in particular). Kolarbyn has its own sauna hut floating on the lake (!), which guests can fire up and use as they wish.

If visiting in summer, don't forget to pack some insect repellent for the mosquitoes.

Open Apr–Oct. Per person: 29 USD (250 SEK). Members of Hostelling International get a 6 USD (50 SEK) discount. Breakfast: 8 USD (65 SEK). Sleeping bag rental: 6 USD (50 SEK); reserve in advance.
+46 (0)70 400 7053
www.kolarbyn.se

Things to do

Fishing on Lake Skärsjön
The lake behind the Kolarbyn huts is full of fish, such as perch and pike. Whether skilled angler or complete beginner, everyone has the chance of making a catch under the expert guidance of Ingmar Johansson. Ingmar invites fishing fans to join him in his boat on Lake Skärsjön.

After choosing your bait, you need only cast your line and then sit back and wait. Patience is, indeed, a virtue in the fishing world. Later Marcus will help prepare the catch to be grilled over the campfire for dinner.

A day's fishing with Ingmar including equipment: 95 USD (800 SEK); half-day: 60 USD (500 SEK). More experienced anglers can purchase a family license in Skinnskatteberg for 9.50 USD (80 SEK) which is valid for fishing in several neighboring lakes.
Reserve via Kolarbyn

Moose safari
This is a real Scandinavian adventure led by Marcus himself. He takes groups of up to eight people into the dense woods surrounding Kolarbyn on the trail of the "King of the Scandinavian Forest." Hoof prints, bite marks in the trees, and moose dung are all signs of its presence. Marcus attempts to attract the moose by expertly imitating their call. It's a serene yet exhilarating experience to sight one of the dignified animals grazing at twilight in a forest glade. They are nervous beasts and the slightest sound sends them galloping off with a comically lurching gait.

Moose have been spotted on every safari that Marcus has led into the forests around Kolarbyn.

Safari with a night at Kolarbyn, breakfast, and dinner: 215 USD (1,795 SEK); tour only: 120 USD (995 SEK).
Reserve via Kolarbyn

On the trail of wolves
Not far from Kolarbyn is one of the few remaining areas in Sweden that is still populated by Scandinavian wolves. Marcus takes small groups to visit the Wild Animal Research Station in Grimsö. The tour begins with an introduction to the scientists' work at the research station, which aims to study behavioral patterns based on data collected from wolves fitted with GPS transmitters. The tour continues, under constant expert guidance, out into the wolves' territory where tracks reveal their presence. The howling of the pack can sometimes be heard echoing through the forest and is a thrilling experience. Scandinavian wolves are very rare with only an estimated 100 still in existence. A direct encounter is unlikely.

Tour with transportation by minibus from Kolarbyn to Grimsö (around 25 miles [40 km]), a night in Kolarbyn, breakfast, and dinner: 235 USD (1,995 SEK). More information on the research station: http://vilt.ekol.slu.se.
Reserve via Kolarbyn

Above (left to right): reception of Kolarbyn; fishing on Lake Skärsjön with Ingmar Johansson; moose in the forest; Scandinavian wolf

9

VÄSTMANLAND:
SWEDEN

HOUSE ON
A LAKE

"Below the
surface, through
the bedroom's
windows, I can
see the waters of
Lake Mälaren
shimmering with
a greenish hue."

THE UTTER INN (IN ENGLISH: OTTER INN) isn't situated near a lake as you may imagine, nor is it on the shore of a lake. No, this inn can be found smack-dab in the middle of a lake. And better yet — it floats! Staying here means living on, and even under, the water.

The house is actually a tiny wooden cabin painted in typical Swedish style in dark red and white, and is anchored in Lake Mälaren, Sweden's third largest lake. It is rudimentarily equipped with a gas range, canisters of fresh water, and a chemical toilet. It's definitely not for anyone who seeks luxury. Nor is it for the claustrophobic or indeed anyone who isn't physically fit: a very steep aluminum ladder takes you to the bedroom below the water's surface. Those who risk the descent into the depths, however, are richly rewarded.

Ten feet (3 m) below the surface, through the bedroom's rectangular windows, I can see the waters of Lake Mälaren shimmering with a greenish hue. Traces of algae have accumulated on the window and from time to time a few curious fish swim by as if to check me out. It's just like being in an aquarium, only this time — I'm the one in the tank! Pike and striped bass pause

79

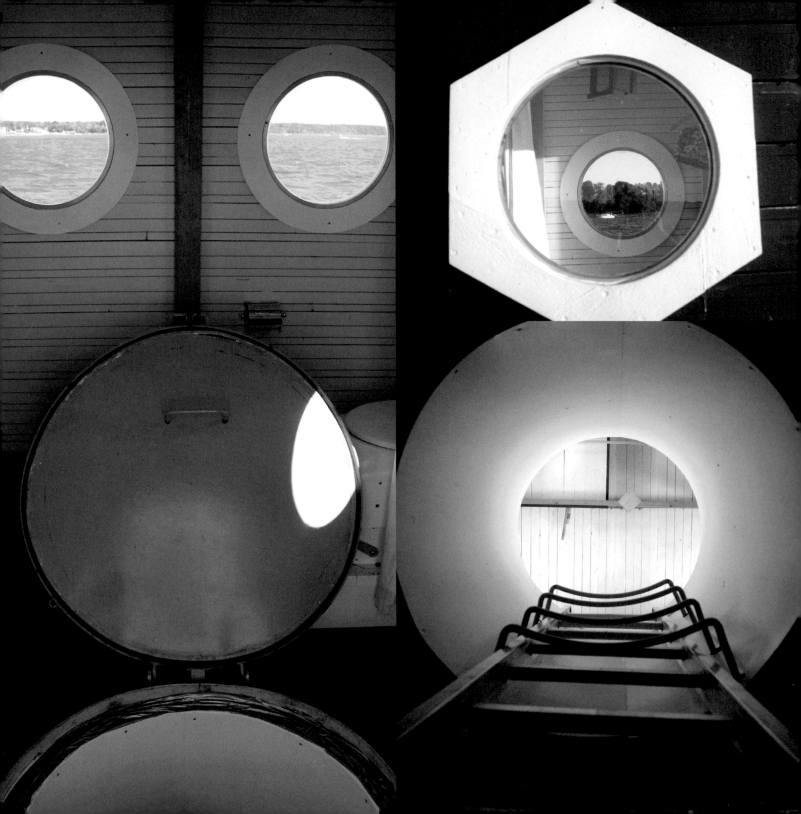

MIKAEL GENBERG, DESIGNER AND OPERATOR

"I couldn't care less whether people call my work art or not. The art is in the eye of the beholder. The experience is the important thing. Only, when you stay at Utter Inn, you automatically become part of the installation."

in the gently flowing current and stare at me unabashedly. And I stare back at them. Who needs a television when you could watch this show for hours and hours?

The lovely weather finally beckons me up and outside. The cabin is surrounded by a terrace-like platform and it's wonderfully relaxing to simply sit outside in a deckchair and enjoy my own mini island on a lake. And this is exactly how you pass the time here. Aside, perhaps, from jumping into the water for a cooling swim now and then or taking the red rubber dingy out for a paddle to the neighboring island. It's perfect for stressed city-dwellers: you can't help but give yourself over to the relaxed island feeling. There is simply nothing else to do here other than listen to the sound of the rippling water and be rocked like a baby with the gentle bobbing of the cabin.

When I open my eyes, there is nothing in sight other than water and on the horizon a small, forested island. Now and then

a motorboat or sailboat pass by and, on the hour, a jam-packed passenger ferry. People on board wave and stare at me with interest as if trying to determine whether I am as crazy as my floating cabin-home. At the Utter Inn you are under constant observation, either from the passing ships above or the passing fish below.

An unexpected diversion arises when a speedboat zooms too close to my island. Its driver waves at me cheerily, totally oblivious to the danger. Fearing the worst, I quickly gather up everything on the table and hold on to it all tightly. Waves surge up violently over the terrace and the whole cabin creaks and tilts alarmingly. Apologizing profusely, the speedboat's driver calls out something in Swedish that must mean "Sorry, I nearly capsized your house!" There's a loud crash inside the cabin — the water container has fallen over. Luckily everything else has been stowed away shipshape and secured as though

preparing for a storm. Then, the excitement is over as quickly as it began and I once again succumb to the meditative powers of the lapping water.

Utter Inn
Mini-island feeling

🔘 Located in the middle of Lake Mälaren, 10 rubber-dingy minutes away from the picturesque small town of Västerås, Västmanland, Sweden. About a 1-hr train ride from Stockholm.

ℹ️ Upper level around 65 sq ft (6 sq m) with cooking facilities, furnished extremely simply. Outside terrace with 2 chairs, a table, and, deckchair. Below deck is larger and cozier with 2 beds, a table, and reading lamps. Light sleepers should not forget to bring earplugs.

Double underwater room with breakfast (but no bed linens): 140 USD (1,150 SEK); luxury option with bed linens and dinner, delivered by boat take-out style: 180 USD (1,500 SEK). Student discount.
+46 (0)21 830 023
www.mikaelgenberg.com

Things to do

Canoe safari on the lake of lilies
This trip is especially spectacular from the end of June and throughout July when the entire lake is carpeted with water lilies. The guide, Daniel Green, has been a passionate birdwatcher since childhood. Sea eagles are often sighted.

Daniel comes to pick up guests from Västerås. Tours Apr–Jul. 8-hr trip: 250 USD (2,100 SEK).
+46 (0)224 740 011
www.svartadalen.nu/eng

Swimming off Östra Holmen
The beautiful wooden ferry *Elba* leaves hourly for the nearby island of Östra Holmen, much loved by locals and tourists alike. This forested rocky island offers plenty of stone bathing spots and a few beaches, including a nudist beach.

Elba ferry departs from Västerås harbor. 10-min boat trip: 5 USD (45 SEK).
+46 (0)21 390 100
www.elba.nu

Vikings at Birka
This day excursion includes a 2.5-hr cruise on Lake Mälaren among an archipelago of idyllic rocky islands, or skerries. Birka is the archeological site of Sweden's oldest and most important Viking trading center and has been designated a UNESCO World Heritage Site. However, as is the case with many archeological sites, the real show lies underground. A handful of booths demonstrate traditional Viking crafts such as blacksmithing and shipbuilding.

Departs Västerås harbor. Tours May–early Sep. Boat trip and guided tour of Birka: 33 USD (270 SEK).
+46 (0)21 390 100
www.stromma.se/en/skargard/stromma-kanalbolaget/day-trips/birka

Above (left to right): canoeing on the way to the lake of lilies; swimming off Östra Holmen island; craftsman at Birka carving a bone knife handle; reconstructed Viking jewelry

10

ISLE OF MULL:
SCOTLAND

CASTLE

"Glengorm has many faces … but the castle is most striking when beset by the mist and rain that bathe it in mystery and suspense."

ONCE UPON A TIME ON A RUGGED ISLAND FAR, FAR AWAY there lived a gentleman and his young wife in a beautiful castle overlooking the sea. Every day, the young lady could be seen pushing a lavender-colored baby carriage down to the harbor of the little fishing village for her children to play in the sand with the local children. In particular with one vivacious little girl.

Time went by and the children of the castle grew up; one by one they left home for the big, wide world. Until one day it was the turn of the youngest child, now a fine young man, to leave home. He went to the big city to seek his fortune, but no matter where he turned, he simply couldn't forget his rugged island and the little girl who he had played with on the beach.

When he couldn't stand it any longer he returned to the island to search for his favorite childhood friend. Hunting high and low he finally found her in a little cottage down by the harbor. She had grown into a beautiful young woman, and, falling down on one knee, he asked her to marry him. From that day on they lived happily ever after in the castle as man and wife.

And today, when the weather is fair, the young wife can be seen pushing a lavender-colored baby carriage down to the harbor for her children to play in the sand with the boys and girls of the village.

This could be the *Tale of Glengorm Castle*, except it is (more or less) true.

A winding road leads from the fishing village of Tobermory to Glengorm, on the most northerly headland of the Isle of Mull, one of the dramatic islands that make up the Inner Hebrides off the west coast of Scotland. The castle itself is like something from a fairy tale with its majestic turrets and crow-stepped gables, and is surrounded by pungent rhododendrons bordering a well-kept lawn. The backdrop is the Atlantic ocean, the peninsula of Ardnamurchan, and, in the far distance, the neighboring islands of Coll, Muck, and Eigg.

I ring the heavy iron bell and the man of the house himself, Tom Nelson, opens the door. He's surprisingly young, somewhere in his late 30s, and although his casual, checkered shirt and corduroys aren't quite the typical attire of the laird of the castle, his impeccable manners are perfectly gentlemanly. Pleasantly unpretentious, Tom seems very down to earth. This may be

TOM NELSON, "LORD OF THE CASTLE"

"I was born in Glengorm and my castle is my home. That's why we don't like having butlers fussing about. We want our guests to feel free to make themselves comfortable, to enjoy the house and its surroundings. They can light the fire and help themselves to a glass of whisky. This isn't a typical boutique hotel, because it is still our family home."

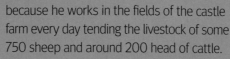

because he works in the fields of the castle farm every day tending the livestock of some 750 sheep and around 200 head of cattle.

Tom apologizes for the stray Wellington boots and badly parked toy tractors and shows me around the castle. Antique rugs and over-sized oil paintings in styles varying from Realism to Abstract vie for my attention. In fact, the castle itself almost resembles an art gallery. Tom's mother is a passionate painter and some of the paintings that adorn the walls are her handiwork.

The castle also caters to the other senses: huge vases stuffed with lilies fill the air with their intoxicating scent. Tom shows me the rooms, moving first to the reception hall with its cozy armchairs pulled up to an open fire. On the wall is a painting of Tom's wife, Marjorie, dressed in deep red, her fur hat and muffler lending the scene a certain *Dr Zhivago* air. In front of the fireplace the obligatory castle hound lies draped across the hearthrug thumping his tail at me in a languid greeting.

In the library a couple from Oregon are enjoying a crackling log fire and a glass of whisky. The well-filled antique bookshelves are a bibliophile's dream. On a silver tray in the corner, an impressive collection of whiskies invite guests to taste a few different Scotches before deciding upon a favorite. This is generally considered a fitting pastime when the weather turns decidedly *Scottish*!

The bedrooms are treasure troves of lovely antiques, some of which are obviously family heirlooms. The décor, far from the sleek minimalism of many modern hotels, is playful and traditional: silver mirrors and bowls, antique secretaries, heavy armchairs, and four-poster beds decorate the rooms. The printed wallpaper depicts tales of dashing Victorian youths courting their coy damsels.

The centerpiece of the ample dining room is the impressive 16th-century table laden with shining silver cutlery. What better way to start the day than to soak up the spectacular views from the enormous windows and indulge in a hearty Scottish breakfast? The dining room looks out onto green fields lightly dotted with white sheep and the shimmering Atlantic beyond. The castle, and also the affiliated café, serve the farm's own organic produce. At breakfast the fruit salad is made with delicious fresh fruit handpicked from around the castle grounds.

Tom's "organic" management style is perhaps inspired by his mother, who strove for a more wholesome lifestyle at Glengorm and hosted spiritual workshops here. Indeed, the area has long been associated with the metaphysical. Not far from the castle there is a small ring of standing stones or megaliths, just like a miniature Stonehenge. They're relics left behind by druids who, 4,000 years ago, used them for mystical rituals. Nowadays it's the shaggy Highland cattle from the farm that wander among these ancient monuments.

Glengorm has many faces. In the sunshine it is imposing yet inviting, especially when the rhododendrons flower in spring, or in August when the heather is in full bloom. But the castle is most striking when beset

by the mist and rain that bathe it in mystery and suspense.

It's not far to the wild and craggy coastline. Several paths lead from the castle past windswept trees and moss-covered rocks to the coves, cliffs, and salty ocean spray. Sea eagles, dolphins, and even Minke whales have been spotted here, making this a true nature-lover's paradise.

The closeness to nature combined with the laidback lifestyle of Tom and his family give Glengorm Castle its unique atmosphere. It is easy to indulge in the luxury and elegance of Glengorm, and even to feel a tiny bit royal. Yet it is not a castle that intimidates with pomp. It has not been designed for demanding tourists, nor, having been built in 1863, does it feel old and mouldy. Glengorm is quite simply a fairy-tale castle that you can pretend is your home, if only for a day or two.

Glengorm Castle
Wholesome, antique luxury

 Tobermory, Isle of Mull, Argyll, Scotland. Close to the northeast coast of the island.

5 double rooms. Per room including breakfast: 210–285 USD (140–190 GBP).
+44 (0)1688 302 321
www.glengormcastle.co.uk

Things to do

Gaelic merrymaking at a céilidh

If you want to experience real Scottish hospitality and see how the Scots let their hair down, then visit a traditional céilidh (pronounced "kay-lee").

If you see a group of gray-haired musicians unpacking their instruments — fear not! This is not an evening of music for seniors. The céilidh is the traditional Gaelic group dance that has undergone a renaissance in recent years and is now fashionable among younger Scots with many towns having developed a vibrant céilidh scene holding regular dance meetings. Instruments played at the events typically include fiddles, accordions, tin whistles, flutes, and, of course, the *bodhrán*, a goatskin frame drum.

You dance either in a ring or in a set. It's not essential to know the individual steps in order to take part, although they're quite easily learned and are sometimes demonstrated in advance. The dances themselves vary enormously in speed and complexity depending on the physical fitness of the group. Many of the men, both young and old, wear traditional kilts. A céilidh is about having fun. Everyone joins in to the cheerful and lively music — locals and tourists alike!

In Tobermory, céilidhs are advertised in the high street store windows. You may see posters at Browns, the Co-op, or the Antobar Art Centre, and the staff at the tourist information office down at the harbor

should also be able to help (when the office is closed in winter call the tourist office in Craignure). The entry fee is about 7 USD (5 GBP) and usually includes tea and cake. Audio samples are available at www. scottishceilidhband.co.uk.
+44 (0)1688 302 182 (tourist info: Easter–Oct)
+44 (0)1680 812 377 (tourist info: Oct–Easter)

Countryside ramble to Tobermory via Ardmore Bay

The picturesque fishing village of Tobermory with its colorful little houses around the harbor is definitely worth a visit during your stay at Glengorm. The village may look somehow familiar – the well-known children's TV series *Teletubbies* was filmed here.

The best way to get to Tobermory avoiding the roads is to follow the scenic trail through woodland past the ruins of Panalbanach. Just beyond the ruins, the trail makes a hard left and finally opens out to offer grand views of the Ardnamurchan peninsula. The sheltered Ardmore Bay is an ideal place to stop for a picnic. A "bothy" offers shelter from the rain and on the left of the bay there is a seal-viewing station. Seals are common on these rocky shores, and even dolphins, otters, and whales have been seen here.

Ask at Glengorm for map and directions. Well sign-posted route. Duration about 3 hrs including the detour to Ardmore Bay. Taxi Tobermory–Glengorm: around 12 USD (8 GBP).

Boat trip to see puffins

A special treat for nature lovers is a boat trip around the coast to the now uninhabited island of Lunga, part of the Treshnish Isles, which is also called Puffin Island, just southeast of Mull.

From May until the end of July puffins nest here in the grassy cliffs. These interesting birds with their oversized, colorful beaks are surprisingly docile and there is plenty of time during the two hours on the island to get a closer look and take some nice pictures. These seabirds only lay one egg at a time. Their nests, to which they return each year, are built into cracks in the cliffs, or, using their feet and beaks, they burrow around 3 ft (1 m) or more into the ground. The pigeon-sized birds have remarkable abilities; every winter they fly thousands of miles south to South Africa or sometimes as far as New Zealand. When they return to their nests they're often seen carrying fish in their beaks to feed their young. They hunt fish underwater using their wings like paddles to reach depths of 300 ft (95 m) and more.

The tour includes an hour on the island of Staffa with its cathedral-like, hexagonal basalt columns, which are said to have inspired Felix Mendelssohn's *Hebrides* overture. The trip also includes a visit to Fingal's Cave and keep an eye out for seals, which are often sighted. Skipper Ian Morrison delivers a humorous commentary. Good sea legs are an advantage since these are not placid waters.

Puffin season: April (the birds arrive at sea) or May (start of the breeding season) to August (birds leave

again). Turus Mara Wildlife and Seabird Cruise Tours leave from Ulva Ferry, around 25 miles (40 km) from Glengorm. 6-hr tour including a 2-hr stay on Puffin Island: 65 USD (45 GBP).
+44 (0)1688 400 297, or toll-free within UK: 0800 085 87 86
www.turusmara.com

Above (left to right): view from Glengorm; céilidh dancing; harbor of Tobermory; puffin on the island of Lunga

PINEAPPLE

11

PINEAPPLE

"In the middle of
the two wings is
the spectacular
summerhouse, the
Pineapple itself. It is
a masterpiece of
design, flaunting a
certain pompous
elegance."

CONCEALED BEHIND A TALL, WEATHERED OLD WALL AND SURROUNDED BY WOODLAND, not far from the Scottish village of Airth, stands a fantastic architectural prank. A wrought-iron gate opens onto a straight driveway that leads through some well-groomed parkland. In the middle of the park, enthroned amid symmetrically arranged trees, sits a fruity extravaganza in stone: an enormous pineapple.

It's amazing how plastic it looks, and with what precision every detail of the prickly fruit has been imitated. It makes a truly imposing sight, and although it is a rather pompous architectural gesture, this can easily be excused by the humor contained within the building. This is literally a monumental gag. And one that only the aristocracy could afford.

John Murray, 4th Earl of Dunmore, built the folly on returning from Virginia, USA, in 1776, where he had served as the British colonial governor. Pineapples were such a rare delicacy in 18th-century Britain that they were regarded as something of a status symbol. The Lord was quite the *bon vivant* and had special greenhouses built at Dunmore specifically to grow the indulgent fruit. These, the elongated buildings below the Pineapple, contained a furnace-driven heating system, circulating warm air between cavities in the walls. The Lord must have truly relished serving his guests fresh pineapple direct from the greenhouse – quite a sensation in chilly Scotland! – apparently, he developed the habit of sending the fruit out to friends at least twice a month.

In Virginia the pineapple had another symbolic meaning. There, in the warm climate, the fruit was quite common, and it was a custom for sailors, when returning home safely from sea, to place one on their gatepost as a sign of welcome. Lord Dunmore liked this little ritual so much he took it with him back to Scotland. His sign of welcome, however, was to outclass anything that had gone before: his pineapple measures a grand 50 ft (16 m) and is, without question, the biggest pineapple around – a superlative built very much to the taste of the eccentric Lord.

Today, this stone-carved, aristocratic whim can be rented as a vacation home. The entrance is at the rear of the building and the rooms are situated within the elongated pavilions beneath the Pineapple,

in the one-time gardeners' quarters. On one side of the Pineapple are two bedrooms and a bathroom, on the other the kitchen and a spacious living room.

Everything is tastefully furnished with antiques. There is a pile of wood stacked at the ready for the open fire in the living room and, to set the right mood, historical prints showing hunting scenes adorn the walls. There are also fruity decorations, including still lifes of strawberries and grapes and even pineapple-shaped candlesticks. There is no TV, radio, or telephone to be found, however. The lack of such modern technology certainly makes it easier to forget about everyday routines for a while.

In the middle of the two wings is the spectacular summerhouse, the Pineapple itself. It is a masterpiece of design, flaunting a certain pompous elegance. The architect remains unknown, yet his work shows many fascinating details of architectural sophistication. The building is round like the fruit; even the door and the glass in the tall Gothic windows are convex. The base of each spiky leaf is higher than it appears optically, to make the rain run down the sides. Even the four chimneys are cleverly disguised as decorative urns, and are inconspicuously integrated into the overall appearance.

Inside, the Pineapple is light and unpretentious. Now, as back in Lord Dunmore's day, a set of garden furniture is supplied: deckchairs, wicker chairs, and a table. It's the perfect place to spend a summer afternoon drinking tea and enjoying the view of the park.

Now and again walkers stroll by and stop to read the National Trust's information plate. As I gaze from the window, an elderly couple sits down on a park bench and looks up to admire our fruity home. A rabbit hops across the lawn. A pair of riders rein in their horses for a quick look at the Pineapple before disappearing back into the woods.

There is plenty of wildlife around — apparently deer and wild boar are regularly seen on the estate.

It is peaceful here. I feel as if the clocks have been turned back to another century. Our modern, technological world seems a million miles away. There's a yellowing framed photograph hanging on the bedroom wall. Three smart boys festively dressed in kilts look confidently, almost triumphantly, into the camera. I can just imagine how they would have run around the Pineapple, in spite of their young age, telling off the staff and calling loudly for their tea. And the rest of Lord Dunmore's set, how they would clink their glasses and applaud themselves and their exquisite building ... A quarter of a millennium later I can only agree with them. A toast to the Pineapple! So prickly and proud.

The Pineapple
Eccentric and playful

◉ 7 miles (11 km) southeast of Stirling, in Dunmore Park, near Falkirk, Scotland. Journey by car is recommended. Follow the National Trust signs along the A904, then turn onto a gravel lane (B9124), which enters a wood. Follow the lane until it ends. Instructions are available from the Landmark Trust when making a reservation. The Pineapple is secluded and not easy to find – although a famous landmark, it isn't sign-posted.

ℹ Since 1973 leased by the Landmark Trust, a charity that restores buildings of particular historical interest, and rents them out to vacationers.

1 twin and 1 double room can be rented for 3, 4, or 7 days only. 3-night rental: from 455 USD (314 GBP) to 1,340 USD (925 GBP) depending on season. Further information only in the Landmark Trust Handbook which costs 14.50 USD (10 GBP) plus postage and packaging.
+44 (0)1628 825 925
www.landmarktrust.org.uk

Things to do

Camera Obscura in Edinburgh
In a small tower in the middle of Edinburgh's old town, itself a UNESCO World Heritage Site, is the city's oldest tourist attraction: the Camera Obscura. Bringing tourists into the city for over 150 years, it's a paradise for fans of optical illusion. Lord Dunmore himself would surely have found great enjoyment here. With the use of a special periscope, visitors can watch live images of passers-by in the street below projected onto a large screen. Other optical toys include a gigantic kaleidoscope, the self-proclaimed "world's largest plasma ball," a hologram exhibition and a live webcam of the city, which can be operated by visitors. The roof of the tower is equipped with telescopes and offers fabulous views over the city. It's a fantastic mix of curious toys and hands-on science.

Edinburgh is around 30 miles (48 km) from the Pineapple. Admission to Camera Obscura and World of Illusions: 12 USD (8.50 GBP).
+44 (0)131 226 3709
www.camera-obscura.co.uk

A taste of life in the 18th century
The high times of Lord Dunmore come to life in Callendar House, an impressive mansion house restored in the style of the late 18th century. The mansion lies within extensive parklands complete with its own boating lake. Rooms have been sumptuously reconstructed, in particular the candle-lit kitchen in which the costumed staff prepare original dishes from Lord Dunmore's day over a large open fire. The finished dishes are offered to visitors to try.

Anyone interested in learning more about life in the 18th century can look through the old photographs, maps, and books in the wood-paneled library (appointment needed).

Callendar House is in Falkirk, around 6 miles (10 km) from the Pineapple. Free entry.
+44 (0)1324 503 770
www.falkirkinspired.com/heritage/callendarhouse.htm

Learn to bagpipe in Glasgow
Have you ever wondered what it is like to play the bagpipe, that most Scottish of musical instruments? Anybody who would like to have a try can test the strength of their lungs at the renowned College of Piping in Glasgow, under the close instruction of its expert tutors. Do not expect to be given a set of pipes straight away, however. Before you can start pumping out a tune, you first have to learn on a practice chanter. This is a bag-less pipe with eight holes that is popular for daily practice even with skilled pipers. The chanter gratifyingly reproduces the familiar plaintive sounds of the pipes (audio sample: www.macege.de/scotlandthebrave.mp3).

Experience in reading music isn't required. The chanter has a similar feel to an oboe or clarinet.

Glasgow is around 25 miles (40 km) from the Pineapple. 1-hr lesson with the College of Piping: 20 USD (14 GBP) plus 52 USD (36 GBP) for a starter kit, which includes the practice chanter and music score.
+44 (0)141 334 3587
www.college-of-piping.co.uk

Above (left to right): the Pineapple; tower of the Camera Obscura; Callendar House kitchen and costumed staff; young Scot playing the bagpipes

12

BUCKINGHAMSHIRE:
ENGLAND

GOTHIC TEMPLE

"A splendid dome, decorated with golden mosaics, rises above our heads. We simply stand and stare in astonishment."

OUR TAXI TAKES US UP THE STRAIGHT AND GRAND DRIVEWAY flanked by two stately pavilions to Stowe School, one of Britain's elite private schools. Very exclusive. And very British. At the gate the school porter hands us the key to our abode – tonight we sleep in our very own temple! This, like the school itself, is set within the magnificent grounds of Stowe Landscape Gardens. As we drive on, boys dressed in white race across the lawn on the way to a game of cricket. The pomp and pageantry of the legendary British upper class still appear to flourish within these grounds. It's as if time has stood still. Today, as guests of Stowe Landscape Gardens, we feel as though we've been allowed to join the illustrious set of the English aristocracy.

Driving along winding paths through beautiful parkland – not a single signpost to guide us – we finally turn into a small lane that suddenly widens into an avenue. And there it is – the Gothic Temple. It sits majestically on top of a hill, a single wind-swept cedar tree for company. The mood is that of an old English landscape painting, a Constable perhaps. As we later discover, this is no coincidence.

The ornate building, with its Gothic windows and battlements, appears vast and reverent, almost daunting. We open the solid, metal-shod door and walk into an airy cathedral-like room that is, in fact, much cozier than expected. A splendid dome, decorated with golden mosaics, rises above our heads. We simply stand and stare in astonishment.

The architecture is quite ingenious. The floor plan is triangular, with a pentagonal tower in each corner. The chambers within, however, are circular. On the ground floor there's a well-equipped round kitchen and a bathroom with freestanding tub and colorful stained-glass windows. On the floor above there are two round bedrooms. The living room is in the high-roofed chamber at the center of the building. A first-floor gallery and the glorious dome above accentuate its circular form. The somewhat hallowed atmosphere is tempered by the furnishings: a comfy sofa, a dining room set, and bookcases stuffed full of books on Stowe Park, its history, flora, and fauna, lend a homely touch. French doors allow you to step outside right into the surrounding parkland.

From the first-floor gallery you look down on the living room as if from the gallery of a

theater. Antique desks and stone window seats afford places for creative or contemplative thought. From here the large Gothic windows offer grandiose views of the park. The monuments, lakes, and bridges of Stowe Landscape Gardens were carefully placed to compose a pleasing sight from the temple's windows.

None other than James Gibbs, one of Britain's most influential architects and designer of such masterpieces as St. Martin-in-the-Fields in London, created the Gothic Temple. It was built between 1741 and 1745 as a folly, with little practical use intended. Indeed, this "temple" has never been used as a place of worship; instead it fulfilled a rather more down-to-earth purpose: when Lord Cobham and his distinguished guests were out walking in the park, it offered them a place to shelter from the rain.

The 360-degree panoramic view from the roof above the dome is still an exquisite experience. The Gothic Temple was placed on top of a hill so as to see and be seen.

The building was, to a great extent, a political statement by its commissioner Lord Cobham. Also known as the Temple of Liberty, it was built as a tribute to the democratic ethics of Cobham's Saxon ancestors and is reckoned to be the pinnacle of the decorative – yet pointedly political – architectural features of the gardens.

It was at Stowe where the famous landscape architect Lancelot "Capability" Brown honed his technique of "painting with nature" to perfection. He composed the landscape like an oil painting: trees, monuments, bridges, lakes, follies, and simple open spaces come together to form a visual masterpiece. Brown intended not only to please the eye but also to stimulate the mind. The diligence of the composition is clearly perceptible; it is this that sets the mood and reminds us of an oil painting. The grounds are the very epitome of a grand English garden.

This is truly a magical place, full of hidden meaning, political messages and the charm of the 18th century. The

temple's ambience, its slightly musty smell, ironstone walls, and the absence of television, radio, and even telephone, all help take us back to that bygone era.

The inquisitive looks and questions of incredulous passing visitors to the gardens: "Are you staying here?" and "Is the temple really available to rent?" bring us back to the present. Indeed, this is still a very privileged place to be. The park is a favorite spot for picnics, and the variety of flora and fauna is lordly in every sense: squirrels, herons, coots, moorhens, geese, ducks, swans, woodpeckers, grebes, terns, treecreepers, and kestrels are all found here. There are opulent water lilies, towering reeds, and green willows weeping over blue lakes. This park really is a natural paradise. Nowadays, perhaps even more so than in the 18th century, this is true luxury.

In the evening, when the park closes its gates to the public, peace settles over the landscape. With a last glance out of my bedroom window I see the moon rising over the Palladian bridge – as pretty as a picture.

The Gothic Temple
Natural, historical, elite – and very British

◉ Stowe Landscape Gardens, Buckinghamshire, UK. 18 miles (29 km) north of Oxford. Remote, in the middle of 365 acres (140 hectares) of National Trust parkland. A taxi from Buckingham (around 3 miles [5 km]) costs around 9 USD (6 GBP).

ⓘ The building is administered by the Landmark Trust, a building preservation charity established to rescue historic and architecturally interesting buildings and their surroundings from neglect. Once restored, buildings are given a second life by being rented out to the public. Further information is available in the Landmark Trust Handbook which you can order through the website.

7-day rental of the Gothic Temple (2 double rooms): from 1,150 USD (767 GBP) to 2,450 USD (1,638 GBP) (depending on season). Available for 3, 4, or 7 days only.
+44 (0)1628 825 925
www.landmarktrust.org.uk.

Things to do

Guided tour of Stowe Landscape Gardens
A tour of the grounds with one of the National Trust's enthusiastic guides is a must. The huge park has a total of 10 miles (16 km) of paths and is considered, alongside Kew Gardens, to be one of the most significant English landscape gardens of the 18th century. There are more than 40 rotundas, temples, and statues to discover. Many of the buildings are English Heritage Grade I listed,

meaning they are of exceptional historic interest. Almost all of Stowe's buildings have a special, often political, relevance. The "Circle of Virtue" includes the Gothic Temple and the Temple of British Worthies, which features statues of personalities esteemed by Cobham, including Edward "The Black Prince" and Sir Francis Bacon. This is counter-balanced by the "immoral" side of the park represented, for example, by the Temple of Bacchus and the Temple of Venus with its "Pleasuring Sofa."

Parts of Stowe School can also be viewed. The school occupies the old manor house, an impressive 17th-century building set in the park. Famous Old Stoics as the former students are called, include Virgin boss Sir Richard Branson, actor David Niven, and Prince Rainier III of Monaco.

2-hr guided tour of the gardens (11am and 2pm most days): free for guests of the Gothic Temple. Gardens closed to the public: Mon & Tue.
+44 (0)1280 822 850
www.nationaltrust.org.uk/main/w-stowegardens

Greyhound races
A completely different side to the famously intellectual Oxford can be experienced at the Oxford Greyhound Stadium. Five days a week the tireless and anorexic-looking greyhounds give air to their natural instincts by chasing a fake hare around a circuit.

The crowd bets on its favorite dog, or simply on its favorite number or color. Here you will find a completely different side of British society than at Stowe. The "Ascot of the Working Class" has its own much livelier and louder charm.

Oxford Greyhound Stadium, Sandy Lane, Oxford. Evening races commence at 7pm Tue, Fri, & Sat.

admission: 7 USD (5 GBP) (including racecard). Daytime races commence at 11am Tue, 2pm Sun; admission free, but there is not as much atmosphere as in the evening!
+44 (0)1865 778 222
www.lovethedogs.co.uk

Punting on the River Cherwell, Oxford
Where would Oxford be without its punting, that icon of university life? It's still a common sight to see a student driving his pole into the riverbed, propelling the flat-bottomed punt along the river, while his lazy cronies recline and chat as they go. Punting refers to boating in a punt — a narrow rectangular boat that is a little like a Venetian gondola, and is popular with tourists and students alike. It is probably the most relaxed way to soak up the atmosphere of Oxford.

The boats glide quietly under bridges and beneath weeping willows, past the Botanical Gardens and the famous Christ Church College, on the lawns of which students recline in groups.

Magdalen Bridge Boathouse, picturesquely situated on the Magdalen Bridge, Oxford. Usually open Mar–Oct. 30-min boat rental including map: 21 USD (14 GBP) (a deposit of 45 USD [30 GBP] and a form of ID is required). However, it's not as easy as it looks! You can also let a "chauffeur" do the work, which costs 37 USD (25 GBP) for 30 min and includes a bottle of wine!
+44 (0)1865 202 643
www.touristnetuk.com/wm/magdalen-bridge

Above (left to right): Temple of British Worthies, Stowe Landscape Gardens; greyhound racing in Oxford; punting on the River Cherwell

13

THE HAGUE:
THE NETHERLANDS

ESCAPE CAPSULE

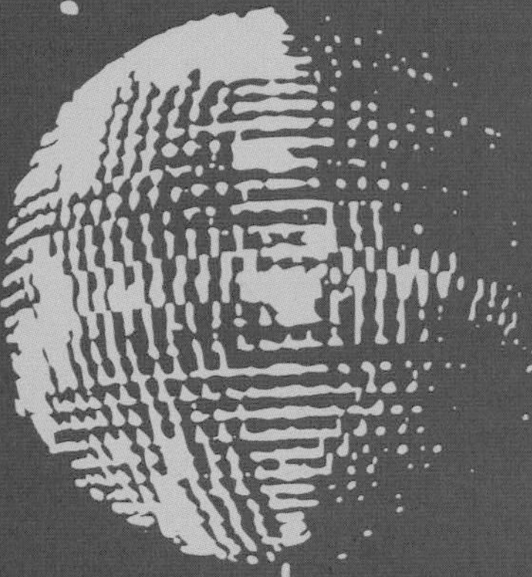

"Inspiration for the
whole idea was of
course the Bond film
*The Spy Who Loved
Me*, at the end of
which Roger Moore
and Barbara Bach
enjoy the privacy of
an escape capsule."

ESCAPE
CAPSULE

A FUNNY-LOOKING THREE-WHEELED VAN APPEARS. A wiry man with prominent sideburns dressed in a boiler suit steps out to greet me. It is Denis Oudendijk, hotel owner and "Scrap Designer" extraordinaire. Fittingly, Denis's van once belonged to The Hague's department of street cleaners. Denis collects things that others have thrown away and converts them or, in his own words, "refunctions" them into something useful. Like his van for example, which he uses for fetching visiting journalists from the station – or any other guest for that matter.

Or indeed like his hotel, which bobs up and down on a canal like something from a low-budget sci-fi film: two luminous-orange flying saucers set against a backdrop of stark Dutch architecture, accentuated by a futuristic round high-rise on the skyline.

I step warily onto one of these floating pods and open a heavy hatch to reveal its interior. I can just imagine the oil-covered men crowding into its confined space. Denis's hotel is made up of two "refunctioned" escape capsules from an off-shore oil rig. As recently as 2000 they were doing their duty on the Ekofisk oil field in the middle of the perilous Norwegian North Sea. In the event of an emergency, 28 men could fit inside – not exactly a comfy retreat. The capsule measures 13 ft (4.25 m) in diameter and wouldn't be considered spacious even for a single guest. Denis has changed the interior as little as possible. Original instructions, in both English and Dutch, for using signal flares and tying knots adorn the walls, designated holes provide a sure-hold for plastic beakers, while reinforced portholes would keep even the roughest seas at bay. Another larger hole, once a more basic version of the chemical toilet supplied today, has been "refunctioned" into a mini-library that contains a few city guides and maps. The simple seat, which runs around the inner wall of the capsule, can be lifted to reveal storage space. Once used for rescue blankets, it has been "refunctioned" into a wardrobe for guests. There's no en-suite here, instead a large container of water must do for washing or making tea and coffee.

An old fisherman's net, found and "refunctioned" by Denis of course, has been fitted with sheepskin rugs – et voilà – it's now the bed. It is surprisingly firm and more stable than a hammock and provides room for two (well-acquainted) individuals.

Denis assures me it has been tested under the most adverse conditions, having successfully held two loads of some 440 lb (100 kg). A red exercise ball serves as a chair, and a plastic globe dangles from the ceiling, along with mugs, a thermos flask, and a glittery disco ball.

A karaoke machine supplies the entertainment: you can sing along to James Bond theme tunes handpicked by die-hard Bond fan, Denis. Happily, there aren't any neighbors to complain about the noise. Inspiration for the whole idea was of course the Bond film *The Spy Who Loved Me*, at the end of which Roger Moore and Barbara Bach, who plays the Soviet spy Anya Amasova, enjoy the privacy of an escape capsule after having saved the world. And, if you reserve the luxurious "James-Bond-Meets-Barbarella" option, Denis will supply you with a DVD player and his entire "007" collection.

Denis's motto is "Regard, before you disregard." Instead of recycling the things he discovers, he looks for a different perspective and gives them a new function. The enigmatic letters "vlnr" on his web page stand for "*van links naar rechts*" ("from left to right") – a different concept from the cyclical nature of re-cycling.

DENIS OUDENIJK, ARTIST AND OWNER

"I was actually looking for a lifeboat when I found the capsules. I couldn't use them to go looking for rubbish along the waterways, as was my original plan, but I loved them so much that I just had to have them. I even lived in them for a while.

You have to give every object a chance. When you find something, listen to it carefully – it will tell you what it wants to be!"

For example, Denis has turned an oven that heats into a ventilator that cools. He calls himself a "City Farmer," regularly scouring the city for useful things that people have thrown away or left behind. He even compiles "Harvest Maps" of what he's found.

To be truthful, the capsule isn't very comfortable. It's not very polished, neither is it luxurious, nor very glamorous at all. But it is authentic, playful, and utterly inspiring. Especially if you meet Denis and get to hear his brilliant neologisms. And the chances of meeting him are high – he likes to greet all of his guests personally.

Carefully dangling my legs over the side of my capsule, I sit and enjoy the gentle movement of the water. The capsule bobs slightly each time a boat passes by. Ducks glide between the water lilies and a cormorant disappears below the water to chase a fish. However, this isn't a place of idyllic beauty.

The whole scene has a more real and unadorned feel to it. At lunchtime, staff from a nearby hardware store wander over to lounge on the shady benches along the canal. Indeed, the busy, industrial character of the neighborhood makes it the perfect home for this escape capsule hotel.

The Capsule Hotel
Rugged, industrial, inspirational

The Hague, The Netherlands. During time of writing, floating in Laakhaven canal. Check website for new location. Further information about Denis Oudendijk: www.vlnr.info.

Contact Denis before arrival. The capsules are mobile and he sometimes takes them with him when he goes to one of his lectures on "refunctioning."
Standard capsule including sleeping bag, "survival breakfast" (orange juice, cookies, energy bar, and instant soup): 90 USD (70 EUR); "James-Bond-Meets-Barbarella" luxury option including an additional silk-lined sleeping bag, DVDs, sheepskin rugs, and bottle of champagne: 200 USD (150 EUR). Students pay less. Bicycle rental is available.
+31 (0)6417 65560 (Denis's mobile)
www.capsulehotel.info

Things to do

Karaoke Taxi

Wannabe pop stars can have a roaring good time on a sightseeing tour of the city in Ton Baggerman's Karaoke Taxi. This rolling entertainment center has a sparkling disco ball, colorful laser lights, and over 500 karaoke videos to choose from. Passengers can belt out their favorite songs to videos displayed on two screens mounted at the back. You can also surf the internet and choose from 22 TV channels.

Taxi operates 7:30pm–8am Tue–Sun. First two kilometers: 10 USD (7.50 EUR); each additional kilometer: 3 USD (2.20 EUR).
+31 (0)900 829 4866
www.karaoketaxi.nl

Bicycle tour of Kinderdijk windmills

The UNESCO World Heritage Site of Kinderdijk offers visitors the chance to see original Dutch windmills at close range. And what better way to do so than in typical Dutch fashion, from the seat of a bicycle. Holland is a paradise for cyclists, with excellent bike paths, often twin-lane and always level, that carry you along the idyllic *grachten*, or canal network. A bicycle tour is an absolute must in the area.

The 19 protected windmills of Kinderdijk huddle together in a relatively small area – a rare sight even in Holland. They were built in the 18th century to pump excess water out of the areas of land reclaimed from the sea, in order to make them agriculturally usable. Eighteen of them are privately owned and inhabited. One of them is open to the public. The area surrounding the mills is a nature reserve where ducks, tourists, and bicyclists vie for space. Peace can be found beyond the open mill.

The Hague to Kinderdijk is 24 miles (38 km). Bikes can be rented from Denis or at the train station in The Hague. Alternatively, for softies, there is a train to Rotterdam Lombardijen (40 min; 13 USD [9.90 EUR] return; www.ns.nl), where you can rent a bike for 8.50 USD (6.50 EUR). Kinderdijk is only 6 miles (9 km) from here. Open mill 9:30am–5:30pm daily; admission 4.50 USD (3.50 EUR).
www.kinderdijk.nl

Visit a Gouda dairy farm

Holland's world-famous cheese is named after the small town of its origin, Gouda. A picturesque bicycle tour takes you from The Hague through fields of green, past cows and fluffy sheep, along pretty canals to the dairy farm Kaasborderij Jongenhoeve. The dairy invites visitors to watch them make the world-famous cheese. Here at the Kaasborderij Jongenhoeve it's still made almost entirely by hand. The hand-made wheels of cheeses are marked with square stamps while factory cheeses, the kind you buy in supermarkets, have round stamps. After five hours of processing, the cheese is ready for drying and ageing. Young and mild Gouda is usually aged for one to two months, while "medium" Gouda has matured for two to six months and has a full, more aromatic taste. The longer the ripening period, the harder and stronger in flavor the cheese becomes.

At the dairy farm every imaginable incarnation of the cheese is available, such as Gouda with tomato, Gouda with onion, or Gouda with olive and garlic. Don't miss the divinely aromatic caraway seed Gouda – delicious!

Gouda is a friendly, touristy city. If you visit on a Thursday, be sure to drop in at the famous cheese market (Kaasmarkt, mid-Jun–Aug only: 10am–1pm Thu) where wheels of Gouda are lined up in rows waiting to be weighed, valued, and tasted.

The Hague via Gouda to the Kaasborderij is around 28 miles (45 km). Bikes can be rented from Denis. The local tourist office can supply a "Fietsgids" (bicyclists' route guide). Alternatively, Gouda is a 20-min train ride from The Hague (7 USD [5.20 EUR]; timetables and map: www.ns.nl). Bikes can be rented from Gouda train station for the 7-mile (12-km) trip to the Kaasborderij. Bike rental is generally 8 USD (6 EUR) per day. Kaasborderij Jongenhoeve farm open 9am–6pm Mon–Sat. Guided tour: 2.60 USD (2 EUR).
+31 (0)182 351 229
www.jongenhoeve.nl

Above (left to right): Karaoke Taxi; riding among the Kinderdijk windmills; Gouda cheeses ripening

14

BERLIN: GERMANY

IN A PIECE OF ART

"Crawling on all fours through low passageways, I am unexpectedly confronted by a skull grinning at me mischievously as if in the knowledge of what awaits me ahead – tonight I sleep in a coffin!"

ON AN INCONSPICUOUS SIDE STREET just off Berlin's resplendent Kurfürstendamm boulevard is the city's most eccentric hotel: the "habitable work of art," Propeller Island City Lodge. Lars Stroschen, a sporty 40-something, is the arty owner and architect behind this mad hotel. He has designed 27 of the most radical rooms ever to have been slept in. It is a live-in art gallery where even the most passive beholder happily becomes an active explorer. Spread across three floors, the hotel is a labyrinth of passageways full of quirky details like distorting mirrors, sinks made from beer barrels, and a very heavy metal lamp that was once part of a railroad track.

The rooms themselves play with the viewer's perception. For example, in the colorful Castle room the pieces of furniture are all buildings; a house in the corner disguises a writing desk, its chimney the seat. In Gallery a rotating circular bed with mounted picture frames offers the occupier an ever-new perspective. Therapy has different colored fluorescent lamps you can switch on and off individually allowing you to mix your own mood. The Symbol room is a great favorite with insomniacs. The

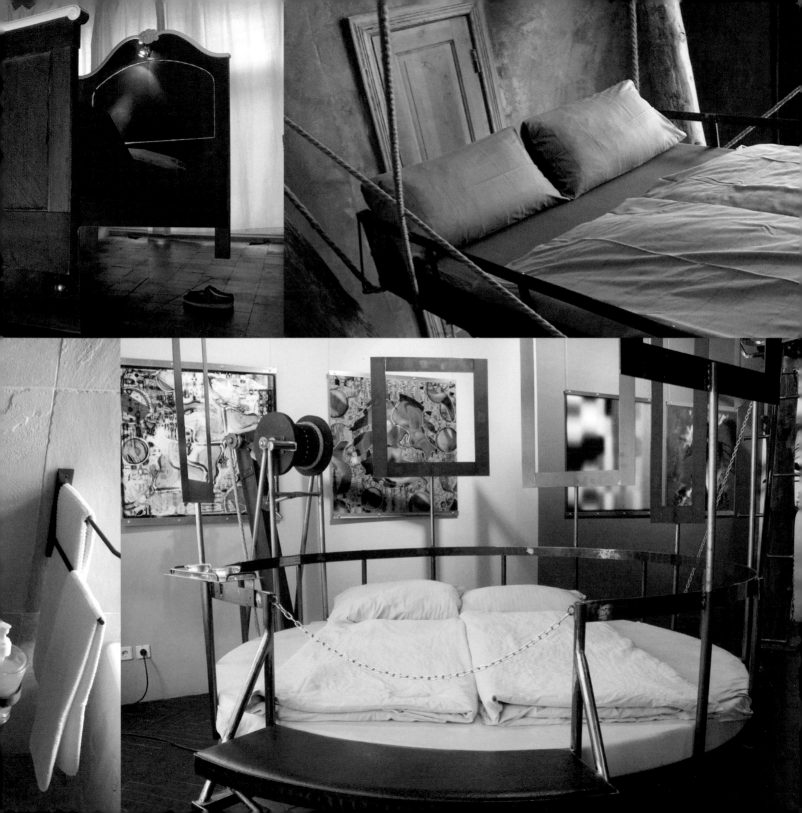

LARS STROSCHEN, DESIGNER AND PROPRIETOR

"The rooms are intended to free people's minds from their preconceived patterns of perception and expectation. Sound is even more powerful than sight in stimulating the imagination. For this reason, I've fitted each room with a soundtrack. I recorded every single sound myself carrying my microphone all over the world from the Mediterranean to Malaysia to collect them."

striking 282 black and white graphic symbols cover literally everything, from floor to ceiling. It's like a giant memory game. Apparently, counting the symbols is as effective as counting sheep – it will have you snoring happily in no time. I am taken to the Crypt and, crawling on all fours through low passageways, I am unexpectedly confronted by a skull grinning at me mischievously as if in the knowledge of what awaits me ahead – tonight I sleep in a coffin! In this morbid bed if you want a particularly peaceful night you can shut the lid. Thoughtfully, Lars has cut out air holes in the shape of a cross to make sure his guests make it through until morning.

Springy floors, padded walls, furniture suspended from the ceiling, a flying bed, and even a room covered completely in mirrors – Lars Stroschen has created something in every guise and for every preference: His rooms are not only designed to please the eye but also the ear. Indeed, for Lars, sound is the crucial element. He initially only rented out rooms to finance his audio experiments, the results of which can now be heard in each of the rooms. By pressing a button on the little control box on the wall you can choose one of six different soundscapes to fit your mood: from waves crashing on the beach or the sounds of the jungle to Lars's own experimental "sound sculptures."

Lars likes to broaden people's horizons and encourages guests to explore the other rooms of the hotel. Open your door and you'll find other doors will be opened to you. You can be sure that your neighbor's room will be so completely and fascinatingly different to yours that you will want to come back again and again – as many do – and test every single room, at least once!

Propeller Island
City Lodge
Informal, industrial, interactive

 On a side street just off Kurfürstendamm in central Berlin, Germany.

27 double rooms, 2 apartments; many have a TV and their own bathroom. Per room based on one person usage: 90–250 USD (70–190 EUR); each additional person: 20 USD (15 EUR).
+49 (0)30 891 9016
www.propeller-island.de

Things to do

Berlin by bike
The alternative way to see the sights of Germany's capital is from the seat of a bike. In groups of up to 15, the Berlin on bike tours follow quiet lanes and bike paths into the hustle and bustle of this surprisingly green and bicycle-friendly city. En route, the tour guides elaborate on the history behind the sometimes magnificent, sometimes crumbling façades of Berlin's landmark sights. There are several tours to choose from. On the Berlin Wall Tour you visit sections of the ruined Berlin Wall with its border crossings, watch towers, and "haunted" train stations while

listening to the stories of bravery and tragedy. The East Berlin Uncovered Tour is also very popular. It offers a glimpse of what it was really like to live behind the Iron Curtain, including a visit to East Berlin's prefab high-rises, industrial wastelands, and the Stasi (secret police) prison and headquarters.

Bike tours are available year-round but are less frequent in winter. 4-hr Berlin Wall Tour: 24 USD (18 EUR). 6-hr East Berlin Uncovered Tour: 29 USD (22 EUR). Includes bicycle hire.
+49 (0)30 4373 9999
www.berlinonbike.de

Swimming on the Badeschiff
Badeschiff literally means "Bathing Ship" and it's just that: an old barge on the river Spree that has been converted into Berlin's uber cool swimming spot. It boasts a spectacular view of the Osthafen harbor and the Alex — East Berlin's landmark TV Tower. In the summer it comes complete with bar and hammocks and an artificial beach. In the winter there's an on-site Finnish sauna and the whole pool complex gets covered with a white cylindrical winter coat making it resemble some kind of fat, floating caterpillar.

It's particularly pleasant at night when the Badeschiff is illuminated, gleaming like a glowworm, and you can soak up the lights of Berlin's skyline while taking a plunge.

Regular events include yoga, DJ parties, and open-air cinema in summer.

Admission for 3 hrs: 16 USD (12 EUR).
+49 (0)30 533 2030
www.badeschiff.de

Tour of the Reichstag
Explore this iconic and spectacular glass-domed building, including the roof-top terrace which offers unparalleled views of Berlin's parliamentary and government quarter. Arrive early to avoid long lines.

Find out more about the history and function of Germany's parliament, including the architecture of the Reichstag building itself, on the free 90-minute guided tour.

Open daily 8am–midnight (last admission 10pm). Admission free. Guided tours: 10.30am, 1.30pm, 3.30pm & 6.30pm. Reservations are required in advance, but if you do wish to reserve at short notice ask if places are available at the West Portal, left entrance (West A), for "Registered Visitors."
+49 (0)30 2273 2152 or +49 (0)30 2273 5908
www.bundestag.de

15

SAXONY: GERMANY

INSIDE A
SUITCASE

·C·MAYER·
BUNDESBAHN·HOTEL MÜNCHEN

"Swinging a cat would
prove troublesome,
but the suitcase
contains everything
you need. I feel
rather cozy lying on
the top bunk under
the home-made
fabric sky."

IT WAS A TYPICALLY UNEVENTFUL NIGHT AT THE STATION NEAR LUNZENAU, a small village in central Germany. Matthias Lehmann, a railroad worker with 25 years' experience in the service of the German Bundesbahn, sat and thought.

Known locally as something of an inventor, Matthias has long been famous for his offbeat sense of humor and his curious creations – like a chair with a seat of nails. His latest invention, however, was going to be very sensible, in a quirky kind of way – The Suitcase Hotel.

Half the village helped build it. The local carpenter made the basic structure while his neighbor, a roofer, created the suitcase-style façade. The village plumber installed the toilet and washing facilities, and to finish it all off, a retired teacher sewed a star-spangled canopy for the ceiling. It took two years of communal effort to complete it – the world's first Suitcase Hotel.

Today the oversized suitcase is a bit of a roadside attraction and passing drivers often drop in to find out what it's all about. Approaching the giant case I find a luggage cart waiting for me. "Particularly useful for female guests who have packed too much ... as usual," Matthias says, winking at me. Well, all I can say is that I am amazed how much *he* has managed to pack into *his* suitcase....

Swinging a cat would prove troublesome but the suitcase contains everything you need. There are two bunks and an old station locker that acts as a cupboard; in the opposite corner there is a sink and even a toilet complete with a discreet warning: "Load Capacity 1,600 kg."

It feels rather cozy lying under the home-made fabric sky, except the ceiling is so low I can't quite sit up straight – which is saying something given my petite stature. So I lie back and focus on what appears to be writing on the suitcase wall. I first wonder if it's the scribbles of bored guests but soon discover that it is, in fact, songs of praise for the hosts' super-friendly service. The wall is their permanently open guest book. One guest sums it up perfectly: "I was here and that is good." For insomniacs, Matthias has thoughtfully provided some bedtime reading guaranteed to lull even the most restless into a peaceful sleep: *The Service Rules and Regulations of the German Federal Railways*.

In the morning, a small breakfast table decorated with handpicked flowers awaits me on the lawn. It's been set with authentic tableware from Mitropa, the German railroad catering company, and overlooks the River Mulde, which meanders past at the end of the garden. This is a truly idyllic spot: birds chirp happily in the trees and a pair of cats stretch lazily before settling down for another nap. The male, after a rather hasty christening, now answers to the name of "Blonde Ingrid."

The Lehmanns' house and grounds are a train-lover's paradise. The suitcase tops off Matthias's unique collection of machinery, tools, and other paraphernalia taken from the railroadman's world. A retired diesel locomotive stands proudly in the garden, while his little shop is packed to the rafters with collector's bric-a-brac. There's even an original wooden station house from the nearby town of Obergräfenhain, which Matthias and his wife Maritta have transported here in its entirety and lovingly restored to its original splendor. Today it houses a tiny museum that holds regular exhibitions of satirical illustrations and caricatures.

MATTHIAS LEHMANN, OWNER
AND BUILDER

"The idea came to me
during a night shift, shortly
after a visiting philosophy
professor had asked if he
could spend the night in my
little station museum. I
loved the idea but sadly it
was impossible because we
regularly hold exhibitions
there. We needed something
else and as my thoughts
went round and round in
my head, my own collection
of 50 suitcases came to
mind. Then it struck me:
what if we had a suitcase
big enough to sleep in?
That was it! I started
planning the Suitcase Hotel
that very night."

Last but not least there's the on-site pub, Zum Prellbock ("The Old Buffer"), which is famous among railroad fans far beyond the borders of Lunzenau. It's a snug little tavern with authentic German railroad tables and chairs. There are ticket-punchers from all over the world on display, draft beer is tapped from a train buffer set into the wall, and an impressive collection of nearly 200 caps from various railroad personnel lines the ceiling. Most of them have a story behind them, Matthias tells me. The red one, for instance, was given to him by the controller of a small station in Sicily: "It was a boiling hot summer's day and for some reason the Snow Waltz was blasting from the tinny speakers. He handed the cap to me, saying, 'This has always brought me luck: it was the only thing to survive a bomb attack on our station by the Red Brigade — luckily, it was my day off.'"

Matthias and Maritta now spend their vacations hunting for rare caps, only visiting countries that aren't represented in their collection.

I sit down at one of the tables beside the river and watch kingfishers flash by in a blaze of blue. The pub's menu ("The Tummy Timetable") offers meals like "From the Steam Boiler," "Porter's Sole," and "Narrow Gauge Salad." As I bite into my "Drive Wheel," a tasty grilled chicken breast with cheese, pineapple, and potato pancakes, I'm addressed by an appropriately unconventional and chatty regular. He looks like a member of the Hell's Angels, but after a while I realize he belongs to a different sort of club altogether: he is a man of God and the local parson. After a pleasant discussion about the pros and cons of monotheist faith, he rushes off to join the ladies of Lunzenau at their weekly choir practice.

I return to my hotel in the garden which is now completely full up — with me, occupying its one and only room.

The suitcase is patiently waiting for me, to take me on a journey to the land of dreams. Despite the murmur of nearby traffic I soon doze off, in the comfortable knowledge that, on this journey, I'm sure to arrive safe and sound.

Zum Prellbock "Kofftel"
Train nostalgia – backpacker-style

🔘 In the garden beside the road running through the small town of Lunzenau, Saxony, Germany. Around 45 miles (70 km) from Dresden.

ℹ️ Two bunks. Per person including breakfast: 20.50 USD (15.50 EUR). Bring your own sleeping bag. Open Apr–Oct.
+49 (0)373 836 410
www.prellbock-bahnart.de (German only)

Things to do

Bake your own gingerbread

The little town of Pulsnitz is famous for its gingerbread (*Pulsnitzer Lebkuchen* or *Pfefferkuchen*), a Saxon specialty. The tradition of making gingerbread dates back to the mid-16th century when the bakers of Pulsnitz first created their secret recipe employing a special mixture of fine spices. In the 18th century they were appointed purveyors to the court of the Saxon king. More recently, during the communist era of East Germany, the Pulsnitz gingerbread bakers' trade was the only one that successfully – and proudly – resisted being turned into a *kolkhoz* (collective) by the regime. Today, alongside a factory, there are eight traditional *Pfefferkuchen* bakeries.

At the tourist office in Pulsnitz you can try making your own gingerbread in their showroom bakery. With the help of an experienced baker, you roll out the ready-made dough and cut it into any desired shape. After ten minutes in the oven, the freshly baked gingerbread cookies can be glazed and decorated with colored icing. Give full reign to your gingerbread creativity! This is a tasty souvenir for all ages.

Around 55 miles (90 km) from Lunzenau, or 18 miles (30 km) from Dresden – take the train from Dresden Neustadt (around 45 min), or drive. Getting there by public transportation direct from Lunzenau is not recommended since it is very time-consuming (around 4 hrs). Pfefferkuchen baking in the Pulsnitz tourist office bakery (Haus das Gastes): 9 USD (7 EUR). Reservations required.
+49 (0)359 5544 246
www.pulsnitz.de – under "Handwerk" (German only)

Ride in the cab of a steam locomotive

If a night in the suitcase has inspired you to take a train ride, join the nostalgic steam train *Lößnitzgrundbahn* as it huffs and puffs its way through idyllic forests and fields and across 19 bridges. Your childhood dreams can come true as you ride squeezed alongside the driver and the stoker in the heat and smoke of the cramped cab. It's like stepping into a scene from a Western with the sweating stoker relentlessly shoveling coal into the blazing fire.

Nowadays the driver is more occupied with slowing down at grade crossings and waving to good-looking mothers and their small children all the while blowing ear-piercing whistles and letting off great clouds of steam from the engine. Last but not least his modern duties include patiently answering questions from curious passengers.

The *Lößnitzgrundbahn* is used by commuters and tourists alike. The hunting lodge and castle, Moritzburg, is a popular stop at about halfway.

The Lößnitzgrundbahn *departs from the station at Radebeul, around 40 miles (70 km) from Lunzenau or 6 miles (10 km) from Dresden. Return ticket Radebeul (Ost)–Moritzburg: 15 USD (11.60 EUR). 7 trains daily. Entire route Radebeul–Radeburg, 10 miles (16.6 km): 17 USD (12.80 EUR). 3 trains daily. Traveling in the cab of the locomotive: 20 USD (15 EUR) extra. Reservation required.*
+49 (0)352 0789 290
www.loessnitzgrundbahn.de

Carving and wood-turning in the Ore Mountains

In Germany, the pretty and colorfully painted Christmas figurines from the Ore Mountains are as famous as Santa himself. The Toy Village of Seiffen is the center for the handicraft of carving and turning wood into beautiful little animals, human figures, and other wooden toys. This village is home to over a hundred wood-turning workshops and five carving studios. It is the only place left in Germany where it is still possible to learn the profession of wooden toy making.

The Toymakers' School opens its doors in the summer vacation to non-students and guests. Instructed by regular teachers, guests can learn to carve a toy horse out of a single piece of wood, or shape a spinning top or snowman. The experts demonstrate how they make the famous Christmas "smoking men" incense burners, wooden animals, nutcrackers, and the "Christmas pyramids," the wooden carousels that turn and jingle in the heat and light of a candle.

The Holzspielzeugmacher und Drechslerschule Seiffen (Seiffen Toymaker's School) is around 30 miles (50 km) from Lunzenau. Getting there by train is not recommended since it is a very slow trip (around 3 hrs). 5-day wood-turning course: 435 USD (330 EUR); 5-day carving course: 200 USD (150 EUR). 1-day courses available on request – phone for details.
+49 (0)373 6066 930
www.erzgebirge.org – click on "Service", then "Ferienkurse" (German only)

Above (left to right): baking mould in the *Pfefferkuchen* bakery; decorating gingerbread; *Loßnitzgrundbahn* steam train; wood-turning in Seiffen

UNDER THE
STARS

UNDER
THE STARS

"Without the walls of
the typical hotel
room I feel somewhat
on show, although I
can't as yet see any
curtains twitching."

IT LOOKS LIKE A TYPICAL MIDDLE CLASS HOUSE ON THE OUTSKIRTS OF BAD LAASPHE, in the depths of Germany's Westphalia. Only an old iron bedstead mounted on the garage roof indicates that it could be a B&B. I peek around the corner – is that really a bed in the garden?

It is! A white iron bed sits on the lawn. A thick, red and white checkered quilt lies on top. Nightcaps have been laid out: white frilly cotton for the ladies and a pointed one for the gents. On a chair beside the bed are a long cotton nightdress and a candle. On the other side there's a vintage-looking milk jug inside of which I find a rather modern flashlight. There's also a nightstand with a jug, a bowl of water, a ceramic bed warmer, and an enamel chamber pot. Ah, the luxuries of days gone by!

The lady of the house comes round to explain a few things to me: in the house there's a bathroom with a shower where I can also leave my luggage. There's a proper toilet, too. If it rains in the night (the sky does look a bit gray already), there's a bed I can use in the house. In this case, it is imperative that I carry the bedclothes and mattress inside, which, she is keen to point out, everybody else has managed to do in the past. After a quick appraisal of my petite stature, she adds that as a last resort I could ring the bell and wake her husband who would then have to come down and help me. Well, I'll just pray for good weather.

She returns to the house and leaves me alone in the garden – my room for the night. Usually the first thing I do when I arrive in a hotel is hang my clothes in the wardrobe, but obviously there are no wardrobes in gardens. Without the walls of the typical hotel room I feel somewhat on show, although I can't as yet see any curtains twitching. In the middle of the garden is a door. It's actually a door to nowhere, or is it the door to my imaginary room? Either way, I won't bother locking it.

I go inside to my closet-cum-bathroom to don my nightdress and then, streaking across the garden, I dive into bed. From my pillow the view of the wooded hills beyond the garden is quite lovely. I haven't been to bed this early for a long time. It's 9pm and cloudy. The clouds paint soft patterns across the darkening sky. Dusk sets in. Bats flutter by and drop into the trees behind my bed. Darkness settles on the garden like a

141

PENSION *Kamerichs*

MARIE-LUISE KAMERICHS, PROPRIETOR

"During the hot summer of 2000 I allowed one of my guests to sleep in the bed on the garage roof. The following morning he was so enthusiastic about his open-air sleep that other guests insisted on having a try. After five others had slept up there, I had to put my foot down! The following year I put a bed in the garden, which was much safer anyway."

blanket and everything is quiet. Even the birds have been silenced by the fall of night. In the far distance a dog barks. Then, again, utter silence. After a short while the first stars prick holes through the clouds and twinkle down at me. I savor the luxury of being able to fall asleep in the fresh air....

It's already light when I wake at 6am, which is a bit early since breakfast isn't served until 8am. I walk across the dew-drenched grass, which is cold and refreshing on my bare toes. Despite the summer heat of July it's quite cool in the mornings, and the bedding that seemed cozy last night has turned clammy.

You can have breakfast outside on the big table or join the other guests, should there be any, in the dining room. At 8am the landlady appears. She's brought me a pair

of wooden clogs to save my feet from the dew. Well, it's a tad late for that, and actually I like the feeling of being in touch with nature. So I stay outside and breakfast at the wooden table, swinging my legs so my toes brush the dewy grass.

Pension Kamerichs
Middle-class adventure

⬤ In the small town of Bad Laasphe, 23 miles (37 km) northwest of Marburg, Westphalia, Germany.

ℹ️ 45 USD (35 EUR) including breakfast, plus 6.50 USD (5 EUR) for salmon, caviar, and a glass of bubbly. A maximum of three beds can be arranged in the garden to suit. Bring a watch if you like to know what time it is when you wake up.
+49 (0)2 752 6120
www.pensionkamerichs.de

Things to do

Dinner down the mine

In the small town of Ramsbeck you can enjoy an unusual take on the candlelit dinner for two: underground in a disused mine shaft! One-time miners invite guests to join them down an old ore mine. The miners' caged railroad wagons carry visitors, dressed in boiler suits and safety helmets, 1 mile (1.6 km) down into the mountain. Dinner is served at the tipping station, a hallway 980 ft (300 m) below the surface. Heavy machinery stands around as if the miners have just stopped for a break. There's even the original 9-ft- (3-m-) long drilling rig which, until 1974 when the mine finally closed, was used to cut dynamite holes into the rock.

The old oil lamps, called frogs, cast their spooky light on our festive dinner of good old mining fare. The miners serve three hearty courses on slate platters in the traditional aluminum mess tins they call *Henkelmänner*, in which their womenfolk used to bring their lunches.

1-hr-20-min drive or 40 miles (63 km) along winding roads from Bad Laasphe. Dress up warm – the mine is around a constant 54°F (12°C). 3.5-hr visit including guided tour, 3-course meal, and a visit to the mine museum: 80 USD (61 EUR). Usually arranged for groups, but on the last Saturday of the month it is available to individuals.
+49 (0)2 9049 7100
www.hotel-nieder.de

Robin Hood in the Sauerland

Have you ever dreamed of stalking through the forest on the trail of wild animals, bow and arrow in hand like Robin Hood? In Brilon, deep in the forests of the Sauerland, animals lie in wait in the undergrowth. Fear not, these wild beasts won't attack. In fact, they don't even flinch as a group of archers approaches, takes aim, and lets their arrows fly – these animals are made of plastic and belong to the Sauerland Archery Club.

This hunting course is for small groups of beginners and experts alike. There are three different routes, each offering both an amateur and a more challenging shot at the 110 animals hidden along the path. Beginners should always be accompanied by an expert or a Club guide.

1-hr-15-min drive or 44 miles (72 km) from Bad Laasphe. Open Wed–Sun: 9am–sunset. The course takes about 3.5 hrs. Day ticket: 10 USD (8 EUR). Club guide (reserve in advance): 25 USD (19.50 EUR) per person. Rental of bow and arrows: 10 USD (7.50 EUR).
+49 (0)1 6042 26448
www.sauerlaender-bogenschuetzen.de

Spa treatment in Germany's largest stalactite cave

The Atta Cave, known as Germany's "King of Dripstone Caves," is a subterranean world of wonder with a twist. Scattered among the many stalactite and stalagmite formations people lounge on deck chairs wrapped in cozy sleeping bags, deeply breathing the clean cave air. At 165 ft (50 m) below the surface, the atmospheric humidity of the Health Grotto is 95% and the air is extremely pure. According to medical reports, spending time here is particularly therapeutic for asthmatics and allergy sufferers. Nowadays cave therapy, or speleotherapy, is an accredited spa treatment. Whether therapeutic or not, even a couple of hours in this colorful tranquillity is extremely relaxing. Wear something warm because the caves have a constant temperature of 50°F (9°C).

The aromatic *Höhlenkäse* or Cave Cheese, the only cheese of its kind in Germany, is ripened in caverns right here in the Atta Cave – a real treat for cheese lovers!

1-hr drive or 43 miles (70 km) from Bad Laasphe. 40-min tour: 9 USD (7 EUR). 2 hrs in the Health Grotto: 12 USD (9.50 EUR). Bring your own sleeping bag or buy one there for a reasonable 38 USD (29.50 EUR). No sleeping bag rental.
+49 (0)2 7229 3750
www.atta-hoehle.de

Above (left to right): tables laid for dinner in the Ramsbeck mine shaft; hunting with the Sauerland Archery Club; relaxing in the Health Grotto at the Atta Cave

17

RHINE VALLEY:
GERMANY

WINE BARREL

"Outside each barrel
hangs a hand-written
notice in golden ink
extolling the virtues
of wine. It certainly
puts you in the right
frame of mind for a
night at the bottom
of a barrel."

AFTER A TIPSY NIGHT IN THE HISTORIC DROSSELGASSE TAVERNS in the famous wine town of Rüdesheim in the heart of Germany's Rhine Valley, what could be more fitting than to sleep off a belly full of wine in an appropriate, if unusual, bed: a wine barrel.

This swinging street attracts tourists from all over the world for its pretty taverns and souvenir stores, which stay open all day and late into the night. Right in the center of the hustle and bustle is an inn called Hotel Lindenwirt, which features a rather unusual array of large barrels hidden in its back courtyard. These oversized, indeed enormous, wine barrels have each been colorfully painted and fitted with two little windows and a rickety door. Until the 1960s, the 80-year-old barrels stood in the Ohlig family's dark and dank cellars and were used in their usual way for fermenting and maturing the beloved grape. Each would hold 1,300 to 1,800 gallons (6,000 to 8,000 liters) of white Riesling or red Spätburgunder — the Pinot Noir of the Rhine Valley.

In the mid-60s, Grandfather Ohlig had a curious idea for his old barrels. He decided not to smash them into firewood as usual,

149

PETER OHLIG, OWNER

"My family and I have a close affiliation with wine. According to my mother I was actually conceived between the barrels! Wine is a delicious indulgence and, moreover, it's healthy! The barrels are meant for those who love their wine so much, they don't want to be too far from it overnight."

but to do something more creative with them. He dragged them up from the cellar to the hotel to clean and restore them. To this day they stand in rank and file decorating the courtyard. Each barrel is fitted with two beds and is named after a vineyard, such as Hallgarten Virgin and Martin's Valley Wild Sow. Outside each barrel hangs a hand-written notice in golden ink extolling the virtues of wine. It certainly puts you in the right frame of mind for a night at the bottom of a barrel.

This could turn out to be a rather sleepless night considering the revelry going on next door. The numerous wine taverns, gardens, and wine cellars of the Drosselgasse not only offer food and drink in abundance, they also host live bands playing cheery folk music. There's lots of dancing, singing, and general merry-making. In truth, the boisterous charm of Drosselgasse may not be everyone's cup of tea, but it is an experience nonetheless.

And it's not only the older crowd, arriving in fleets of buses, who can be seen shaking a leg to the music: the young folk join in, too.

I retire for the night to my decorative barrel, which appropriately carries the name of *Rüdesheimer Katerloch* – a place to recover from a hangover. The interior is simple, yet a shower, WC, and wardrobe have been added at the back. My bed turns out to be rather slim, and probably unsuitable for bigger folk. And what's this? No, not a wine-induced hallucination – the bed is strangely misshapen, widening out in the middle following the contours of the barrel.

Around midnight, as the party music finally fades away, I can hear my barrel neighbors return, talking animatedly. I wonder if it was Diogenes, the tub-dwelling Greek philosopher, who has inspired them in their lively discussion, or more likely, the potent wine of the Drosselgasse.

Hotel Lindenwirt
Simple and rustic

⦿ On Rüdesheim's famous Drosselgasse, within the UNESCO World Heritage Site of Upper Middle Rhine Valley, which is littered with castles and vineyards.

ℹ 6 wine barrels, 2 beds each, and simple furnishings. Per person including breakfast: 45 USD (34.50 EUR). Barrels not available Jan–Feb.
+49 (0)6 722 9130
www.lindenwirt.com

Things to do

Musical wine-tasting at Kloster Eberbach
Situated in idyllic woodland, the monastery at Eberbach offers an original way to taste wine. A cultural history tour around the ornate Cistercian monastery traces the footsteps of the Eberbach monks through its venerable cloisters. The guided wine tour has six stops, including the historic Cabinet Cellar, which is the origin of the Kabinett classification in German wine-making, and the Monks' Dormitory with its cross-ribbed vaults, world-famous as the library in the film of Umberto Eco's *The Name of the Rose*. At each stop a choir or flute duo provides a musical accompaniment, while a selection of the monastery's fine wines are served. The first vines were planted on the hillsides surrounding the monastery some 800 years ago. This was the birth of viniculture in Rheingau, Germany's predominant wine-growing region.

The domain and vineyards of Kloster Eberbach, including those in Rüdesheim and Assmannshausen, constitute the largest vineyard domain in Germany.

Kloster Eberbach is 7.5 miles (12 km) from the wine barrels. 2.5-hr musical wine-tasting (German only): 32 USD (25 EUR); tour without music: 26 USD (20 EUR). The tours are held at irregular intervals. Reserve early!
+49 (0)6 723 9178 111 (or -112, or -113)
www.klostereberbach.de

A boat trip along the Middle Rhine
A boat trip is, without question, the easiest way to see the spectacular castles that cling to the high cliffs all along the picturesque Upper Middle Rhine, a landscape listed as a UNESCO World Heritage Site. One popular destination is romantic Bacharach, which, according to enthusiastic visitor Victor Hugo, is "one of the most beautiful towns on Earth." The restored timber-framed houses, the old defense turrets on the town wall, which is still walkable, and the towering Castle Stahleck all give Bacharach a strong medieval feel. Castle Stahleck (now a youth hostel) offers a magnificent view over the Rhine.

Both the Bingen-Rüdesheimer *and the* Köln-Düsseldorfer *boats leave from Rüdesheim and stop at Bacharach. Down river to Bacharach: 1 hr; return: 1 hr 30 min. English-language audio guide on board.*

Return trip on Bingen-Rüdesheimer*: 16 USD (12 EUR).*
+49 (0)6 721 14140
www.bingen-ruedesheimer.com
Return trip on Köln-Düsseldorfer*: 19 USD (14.40 EUR).*
+49 (0)2 212 088 318
www.k-d.com

Romantic tour of the Rhine and Castle Rheinstein
Take a day trip to see the highlights of the Rüdesheim area, including the Rhine Valley, its numerous vineyards, and a medieval castle. In Rüdesheim a cable car takes you right over the vineyards up to the imposing Niederwalddenkmal monument with its 40-ft (12.5-m) statue of Germania. From there, a trail leads on for about 2.5 miles (4 km) through sparse woodland via the ruins of Fort Rossel and the Zauberhöhle cave to follow a section of the Rheinsteig long-distance walking trail to the old hunting lodge, Jagdschloss Niederwald. A chair lift returns you comfortably to the small town of Assmannshausen, which is famous for its red wines. There is a ferry across to Castle Rheinstein on the opposite bank. This medieval castle, with its suits of armor, castle chapel, and lady's chambers, is open to the public. After your visit catch the ferry back to Rüdesheim.

"Romantikticket" including cable car, chair lift, ferries, and admission to the castle: 16 USD (12 EUR). A route map is available online or at the cable car station.
+49 (0)6 722 2402
www.seilbahn-ruedesheim.de

Above (left to right): evocative musical wine-tasting inside Kloster Eberbach; entrance to Hotel Lindenwirt; cruising along the Rhine; Castle Rheinstein

18

CIRCUS WAGON

"Deep in the Arcadian beauty of the Beaujolais with its softly rolling hills, three historic *roulottes* or gypsy wagons stand in a luscious meadow."

IT'S THE CLASSIC CHILDHOOD DREAM: JOIN THE CIRCUS AND LIVE LIKE A GYPSY. Here today, gone tomorrow, with only a caravan to call home. Die-hard romantics still hoping to fulfil this dream can do so, at least for a few days, in La Serve in southwest France. Deep in the Arcadian beauty of the Beaujolais with its softly rolling hills, three historic *roulottes* or gypsy wagons stand in a luscious meadow among trees brimming with apples. In autumn, when the fruit falls to the ground, the wagons look as though they're set among rosy-red splodges of paint on a rich green canvas.

These wagons have retired from their life on the road and, with their wheels standing still, offer accommodation for guests to La Serve. The lives of owners Pascal and Pascaline Patin have also reached a peaceful phase after many years of youthful travel and adventure abroad. Having bought their manor house in La Serve, they now work full-time at restoring these wagons. It's their "stationary journey," as Pascal likes to call it. He repairs and refurbishes original examples of the nostalgic vehicles and also builds brand new ones in vintage style. Guests are welcome to visit him in his workshop below the breakfast room and watch him work.

In the restoration of the three original wagons, Pascal and Pascaline have paid great attention to every little detail. There are beautiful built-in Art Nouveau cupboards with fine curved doors, an original (though no longer functioning) wood-burning stove shining proudly in a corner, rich claret-colored brocade, velour and velvet furnishings that shimmer along-side lacy curtains and yellowing photographs of the original inhabitants adorning the walls. Together they create an air of luxurious and opulent nostalgia. Quite a few of the decorative pieces are personal souvenirs from Pascal and Pascaline's travels through Asia, particularly in the Roulotte des Étoiles, which flaunts a distinctive Oriental ambience. In front of each wagon a table and chairs provide a fabulous picnic space while a couple of deckchairs afford a place to relax and soak up the sun.

Each wagon has its own atmosphere. The Roulotte des Amoureux, built in 1920, is petite, fanciful, and very homely – just like a little nest – with a cozy double berth, extra cot, and dainty little chairs. The Roulotte de Manège, from 1950, is more rustic and spacious with a separate bedroom and the original, decorative stove.

157

PASCAL AND PASCALINE PATIN, PROPRIETORS OF LA SERVE

"We've always dreamed of living in a circus wagon. If you get tired of your present location you simply pack up and move on to the next one. In France the *roulotte* has always been a symbol of nostalgia and freedom. When we found this house, we settled and began to re-develop it. Our original vision of living on the road hasn't really worked out, but now at least our guests can, if only for a few days, live our dream for us."

Genuine photographs of circus folk, the one-time owners, embellish the walls. The Roulotte des Étoiles, built in 1900, is the oldest and largest of the three wagons. It once belonged to the famous Bouglione Circus and is outfitted with lavish Eastern furniture and a lot of gold and glitter. Ornate doors and romantic star-shaped lights set the tone and the air is perfumed with Oriental fragrances.

Staying here is a bit like camping. You meet other guests on the way to use the facilities in the main building and in the morning you shuffle through dew-drenched grass to breakfast, which is, by the way, delicious. It includes home-made jams and freshly baked bread, the delightful smell of which regularly wafts across the meadow.

This is a happy, peaceful little place: horses browse in the meadow, sheep graze in the field next door, and even the numerous cats and dogs play together amicably. The rustic, stone-built main house incorporates many different styles and flavors, each a contrast to the next, yet harmonious in their whole. An abundance of north European flowers flourish in front of an extravagantly carved wooden veranda from India and, behind that, Tibetan prayer flags flutter on the soft breeze. It's a beautiful symbiosis of Asian spirituality and French laissez-faire.

Dreaming of journeys to faraway and exotic lands is easy here. Without doubt this is the spiritual birthplace of many voyages, first inspired by a stationary journey in the *roulottes* at La Serve.

Les Roulottes
Nostalgic and fanciful: a harmonious cocktail of cultures and styles

◉ La Serve, 69860 Ouroux, France. Tip: use the zip code to find the right Ouroux since there are two others in the vicinity! Set in a beautiful, tranquil area a stone's throw from the vineyards of the Beaujolais.

ℹ️ Roulotte des Amoureux: 65 USD (50 EUR); Roulotte de Manège: 75 USD (55 EUR); Roulotte des Étoiles: 80 USD (60 EUR). Including breakfast. Bring your own towels and rubber boots.
+33 (0)4 7404 7640
www.lesroulottes.com

Things to do

Historic Cluny and the St James' Way
The town of Cluny, with its majestic monastery, has been a gathering point for pilgrims on the St James' Way since the 11th century. It is one of the northern starting points for the famous spiritual journey to Santiago de Compostela in Spain.

Cluny is about 22 miles (35 km) and about two days' march from La Serve, the pilgrimage route passing close by. For a day trip, there is a pleasant roundtrip from Sainte-Cécile to Cluny via the village of Jalogny. The route runs along a quiet back road in lovely countryside, across fields, through woodland, and over gentle, green hills before reaching the famed town of Cluny.

In the Middle Ages the influence of the Benedictine Cluny Abbey reached across the whole of Europe. To this day the town is dominated by the history of the once powerful and mighty abbey and tourists swarm here to visit its Romanesque ruins.

For a "spiritual" break of another kind drop in at the old abbey cellar where local wines and brandy can be tasted. Those seeking a deeper spiritual experience can continue a further 5 miles (8 km) on foot or bicycle along the trail known as the Voie Verte to the ecumenical Christian community at Taizé. From Cluny the journey back to Sainte-Cécile follows the long-distance hiking trail GR76, which, in this section, is also part of the St James' Way route.

Sainte-Cécile is 15 miles (25 km) north of La Serve. Trail from Sainte-Cécile to Cluny and back is 14 miles (22 km). Le Cellier de l'Abbaye, Cluny, wine and brandy tasting: around 10 USD (7.50 EUR) donation.
+33 (0)3 8559 0400

Secret silk weavers' passages of Lyon
In 1540, the French King Francis I issued a charter giving Lyonnais silk weavers the monopoly on silk and brocade production in France. By the time Joseph-Marie Jacquard (1752–1834) had invented his punch card loom mechanism in the early 1800s – an incredible improvement – there were 120,000 working silk looms in Lyon.

Today, the workshops, steps and narrow passageways, hidden in the Croix Rousse quarter, offer a fascinating testimony to the once extremely hard lives of Lyon's silk weavers, or *canuts*.

At La Maison des Canuts (The House of Silk Weavers), the complicated and exceedingly laborious technique of silk weaving is demonstrated. The work requires a high level of concentration especially since the weaver sees only the rear side of the cloth. In a single strip of silk approximately 30 inches (80 cm) in width around 7,000 fine silk threads are used. If 15 colors are woven 35 loom shuttles may be used to carry the weft (horizontal threads) through their labyrinth of warp (vertical threads). If any one of the extremely delicate threads breaks, it reduces the value of the entire cloth.

To aid the craftsmen in delivering their silk quickly and, more importantly, out of the rain, to the traders in the lower part of the city, a large network of traboules were built. These are covered gangways, stairwells, and hidden passageways that run as short-cuts below the streets of Lyon. During World War II, they were successfully used by

the French Resistance to thwart the occupying Nazis. There is a 1.5-hr guided tour in French of the *traboules*. Alternatively, you can explore them on your own following signs that show the way. Maps of the *traboules* can be obtained for free at the tourist office.

Lyon is around 40 miles (64 km) from La Serve. 45-min guided tour of the silk weavers' house (French only): 8 USD (6 EUR); combined with additional 1.5-hr tour of the traboules: 12 USD (9 EUR).
+33 (0)4 7828 6204
www.maisondescanuts.com

Home cooking – the French way

In country kitchens around Beaune, connoisseur, sociologist, and experienced *chef de cuisine* Alex Miles offers an insight into the French love of food.

The half-day course, held in English, begins with a morning visit to the local market to pick ingredients, design the menu, and chat to the stall holders, who all seem to be on first-name terms with the jovial cook. Then the cooking can begin! Back in the kitchen, American

expatriate Alex prepares dishes that ordinary French people cook at home. These include meaty stews, delicate vegetable dishes, and creamy desserts. The aim is to demonstrate some simple yet delicious recipes that can be easily recreated. Those who wish to help are welcome to do so – too many cooks don't spoil the French broth. The lesson ends with a lunch of what has been prepared.

Alex operates out of different locations all within around 5 miles (8 km) of Beaune, 62 miles (100 km) from La Serve. Half-day cooking course with 3-course lunch: 200 USD (150 EUR) per person for 6–14 people; 240 USD (180 EUR) per person for 4–5 people.
+33 (0)3 8074 0363
www.miles-alex.com

Above (clockwise from left): wagons in the apple orchard; authentic stove in the Roulotte de Manège; bedroom of Roulotte de Manège; traditional Burgundian appetizer; Lyonnese silk bobbins; Romanesque turrets of Cluny Abbey

19

LUCERNE:
SWITZERLAND

PRISON CELL

"Nowadays, it's no longer dangerous criminals who skulk behind these barred windows, staring with longing at the outside world; guests from all around the globe come and go at will."

"THE PRISONER IN CELL 4, ANTON, WAS ALWAYS DEMANDING SPECIAL TREATMENT. For instance, he wanted to be moved into a community ward with other prisoners. He would threaten us, saying if we didn't consent to his wishes, he would do terrible things, even kill himself. After a while we stopped taking it seriously. Until one day he demanded an extra ration of cigarettes and, to emphasize the point, he cut off his earlobe with a razor blade and handed it to me. It was quite a traumatic experience. He got his cigarettes that time, but thankfully, his tantrums subsided shortly after that."

This is one of many true stories you can read about at the district prison in Lucerne. Each prison cell has an inscription on the wall relating the story of one of its past occupants, as seen through the eyes of their wardens. Nowadays, it's no longer dangerous criminals who skulk behind these barred windows, staring with longing at the outside world; guests from all around the globe come and go at will. The prison hotel is located in the picturesque quarter of Old Town Lucerne, only a few minutes from Chapel Bridge, Lucerne's famous landmark, and Lake Lucerne at the foot of the Swiss Alps.

Up until 1998, this impenetrable gray building with its many barred windows was home to up to 55 prisoners. Since then much has changed, most importantly, a little thing called comfort has come to stay. The cells have been renovated and now boast parquet floors and en suite bathrooms. The spartan, minimalist furnishings appeal particularly to younger visitors. Undeniably, the hotel still has an air of the corrective institution about it and it's quite intentional, as I realize when I'm greeted at reception by staff wearing their striped convict's uniforms. Without a doubt, the memories of past crimes still waft through the barred windows and along the long, bleak corridors. These ominous gangways are T-shaped, which made it easy for one warden to keep an eye on three corridors at once.

Display cases are filled with curious prison paraphernalia: a hot water bottle with a built-in clock, a typically overlarge prison keyring, and a straitjacket with seemingly endless sleeves. The hotel rooms have kept most of the original fixtures: the very heavy door to my room dates from 1863 and still has its multiple bolts — even the metal bed frame is original. The special suites hold even more memorabilia; an elaborately

AFRIM BAFTIROSKI, PROPRIETOR

"Nowadays you have to offer something special to differentiate yourself from the competition. That's why I took on the Jailhotel. I hope it will help couples to make up after an argument: 'Darling, I really am sorry. I'd go to jail for what I did.... Wanna come too?'"

carved gentleman's wardrobe, once used by the prison director, covers an entire wall of the Director's Suite while the Library Suite — I can hardly believe my eyes — holds the original books from the prison library. Titles deemed suitable for the inmates include *Kill with Kindness*, *The Hangman's Whip,* and *Murder is Easy*.

Particularly remorseful guests can book the "Guilt and Atonement" special. On arrival, the repentant guests are given original striped prison uniforms to wear and are frog-marched in handcuffs to a cell, where a frugal meal of bread and water awaits them. The hotel's concept has particular appeal for the young and the young-at-heart — on the way to the bar, I pass a group of young men playing an animated game of table soccer. The hotel bar, styled in neon blue, is open every evening and is a favorite with Lucernians. Thursday is disco night so

you might want to reserve a room facing the prison courtyard.

This hotel is so authentic you cannot escape the feeling that what is an amusing distraction for us now was a bitter reality for inmates not long ago. The prison, now so comfortable, was once a place where crimes — which the average good citizen usually only encounters in books and movies — were a real part of life. My mind starts to wonder what it would be like if I had to spend the rest of my life in this prison cell. And so I feel very glad and relieved that I can escape for a day trip to Lake Lucerne. On leaving, I see I've left my window open. But then I realize it doesn't matter — if you can't break out, then you can't break in. Out in the street, a joyous sense of freedom washes over me. This hotel certainly gives you a renewed appreciation for the pleasures of life — especially when checking out.

Jailhotel Löwengraben
Austere, young, steeped in history and fate

In the center of Old Town Lucerne, close to the lake, Switzerland.

Depending on season, standard cell for 2 people: 72–132 USD (80.50–149 CHF); suite for 2–3 people: 115–248 USD (130–280 CHF). Includes breakfast. "Guilt and Atonement" special with original prison uniform, bread, and water: 8.50 USD (10 CHF) surcharge.
+41 (0)41 410 7830
www.jailhotel.com

Things to do

Alphorn lesson
Urs Patscheider, a genial old gentleman with a Santa-like beard, has been playing the alphorn for over 40 years. Novices are invited to join him for a master class and anyone who fancies having a try on the 11-ft- (3.5-m-) long instrument is welcome to do so. Up on the idyllic Alpine pastures, with a view across Lake Lucerne, the alphorn is blown like a trumpet, and with Urs' help everyone achieves at least one note out of it. Available also in combination with a walking tour.
45-min trial lesson: 43 USD (50 CHF).
+41 (0)41 320 6834, cell +41 (0)79 670 9794
(Urs doesn't speak English)

Treading in the footsteps of William Tell
A romantic trip across Lake Lucerne in a paddle steamer takes you to Tellskapelle (Tell's Chapel) where a particularly beautiful section of the long-distance hiking trail, the Swiss Path, begins. Here, the hiking path runs along the "Urner Becken" section of the lake. It leads for 22 miles (35 km) through areas of exceptional natural beauty, affording breathtaking views of the peaks and lakes of central Switzerland. Tell's Chapel is a monument to the legendary Swiss hero Wilhelm (William) Tell who, during a storm, supposedly leapt from the boat of his tormentor, the bailiff Hermann Gessler. Managing to escape to the shore, Tell emerged on this very spot. Next to Tell's Chapel stands Switzerland's largest set of carillon bells. You can operate the bells to play one of 20 different melodies in the ten minutes after every hour.

The Swiss Path continues from the chapel following the shore of the lake, crossing wooden footbridges, climbing steps, leading down through a small tunnel, and up to several viewpoints, including the one at Morschach with its view of the famous Rütli Meadow opposite. This Alpine meadow is drenched in mythology; it is said to be here that the Rütlischwur oath took place – this is the very birthplace of Switzerland, where its founders swore their allegiance to the Swiss confederation. The Axenstein-Känzeli viewpoint also offers a glorious vista across the lake to the Pilatus mountain. The path ends in the pretty little vacation village of Brunnen where the paddle steamer docks on the promenade to take you back to Lucerne. This is a ramble through truly dramatic and breathtaking scenery.

Swiss Path: Tell's Chapel to Brunnen takes around 5 hrs; other walking combinations are possible. Paddle steamer return ticket: 50 USD (58 CHF); 2.5 hrs each way.
+41 (0)41 367 6767
www.lakelucerne.ch

The world's steepest cogwheel train
The classic cogwheel railroad tour begins by first crossing Lake Lucerne by boat to Alpnachstad. From here, the world's steepest cogwheel (rack and pinion) railroad, which was built in 1889, climbs a 48% incline to the peak of the Pilatus mountain. At 6,994 ft (2,132 m) a spectacular panorama awaits with several hiking trails of diverse lengths and difficulties to choose from, some of which have been blasted into the side of the mountain. Alpine ibex and marmots can often be spotted up here. To return to the valley, you can take the gondola cable car to Kriens, and from there the bus back to Lucerne.

The cogwheel railroad is open from May–Oct or Nov, depending on the weather. "Golden Round Trip" ticket including boat trip across Lake Lucerne (1.5 hrs to Alpnachstad), cogwheel railroad to the top of Pilatus (30 min), gondola cable car back to Kriens (45 min), and the bus from Kriens back to Lucerne (15 min): 60 USD (72 CHF).
+41 (0)41 329 1111
www.pilatus.ch

Above (left to right): Chapel Bridge, Lucerne; Urs Patscheider demonstrating the alphorn; walking the Swiss Path around Lake Lucerne; the cogwheel railroad climbing Pilatus mountain

20

TICINO: SWITZERLAND

HOTEL IN A MOUNTAIN

"Familiar orientation points, taken for granted in our everyday lives, are missing here. Not even the sun offers its habitual rhythm in this windowless world of rock and water."

"HIGH ABOVE THE CLOUDS. DEEP WITHIN THE MOUNTAIN. AT THE SOURCE OF THE RIVER." That's where this hotel claims to be. It sounds secretive, mythical even. At 6,725 ft (2,050 m) above sea level, its surroundings, the landscape of the St. Gotthard Pass in the Swiss Alps, certainly fits the bill: barren, desolate, and at the mercy of nature. It seems as though only the nearby Lucendro Dam offers any resistance to the elements.

The hotel's entrance is little more than a mere hole in the mountainside. It's hard to believe that a luxurious hotel hides behind the small red door before me. A friendly voice on the intercom bids me enter, a buzzer sounds softly, and a door opens onto a dimly lit tunnel. It's bare, dark, metallic, and damp. I can hear water dripping. The tunnel is a remnant of a World War II military bunker, in those days frequented only by soldiers.

I walk along the tunnel, heading deeper into the heart of the mountain. Along the way there are several heavy steel doors to pass through with yellowing military signs ordering me to shut them securely. As I close each door behind me I feel like I'm shutting out the world a little bit more, as though crossing each threshold is part of an ancient ritual ultimately leading to the innermost sanctuary of the mountain.

Six hundred feet (200 m) into the tunnel I reach a glass door; condensation on the panes lends it the appearance of a living membrane. Beyond it a red carpet can be seen. There's no reception desk — each guest is received personally. A man welcomes me into a spacious cavern: he looks intellectual and agile and seems to glow with energy. It's Jean Odermatt, the founder of this "monastery in the mountain" which is La Claustra.

The atmosphere feels exclusive yet relaxed. A rectangular building protrudes from the rock: "The restaurant," explains Jean. Armchairs and a large vase of lilies stand in the foreground and colored floor lights illuminate the scene. All is carefully composed and uniquely effective in its simplicity — luxury in harmonious contrast with the raw granite of the mountain.

Here, too, a perpetual but soothing dripping sound echoes from the walls, like some esoteric soundtrack. But these drops are real: large clay urns catch them as they fall from the ceiling. Overhead, a reservoir carrying 9,900 gallons (45,000 liters) of

JEAN ODERMATT, ARTIST, SOCIOLOGIST, AND FOUNDER OF LA CLAUSTRA

"It's metamorphoses that fascinate me. How do the clouds and the weather evolve? How can something designed for a military purpose, an artillery bunker, be transformed into a communications station? I see La Claustra as a vessel in which interpersonal processes take place."

the purest drinking water is fed by five natural springs. The Reuss River rises directly above us, and the Rhone, the Rhine, and the Ticino rivers also have their sources here. "The Gotthard massif is one of only three areas in the world from which rivers run in all four directions," explains Jean, "only the Himalayas and the Orinoco region in South America can boast the same."

For Jean, the Gotthard is a magical place. He's been grappling with this landscape since 1983, La Claustra being one of the resulting projects. Not only a watershed, the Gotthard is also a divide for Europe's climates, languages, and cultures. Jean sees it as a place where metamorphoses happen, those of nature as well as of society: clouds change into snow, mountains change into military forts which in turn change into hotels, transportation routes change from high passes to deep tunnels. The newest development is the Gotthard Base Tunnel, which on completion in 2015 will be the longest rail tunnel in the world.

La Claustra is a 13,000 sq ft (4,000 sq m) subterranean world wrought into the heart of the mountain. From World War II until as recently as 1995 it was a secret artillery fortress called San Carlo, and in wartime up to 300 soldiers were stationed here to defend the pass. The military installation has been partly dismantled and partly converted. The once menacing cannons are gone and, fittingly, a telescope has taken their place. Today the facility serves an entirely opposite purpose: communication.

Designed as a kind of post-modern monastic retreat, La Claustra is a place for reflection and contemplation, but also for conversation. It aims to bring together all sorts of different people — scientists, managers, artists, or craftsmen, as well as the odd tourist.

Jean leads me to my room along wooden walkways laid with red carpet. Overhead, white linen canopies catch drops of water. Modern air conditioning ensures a comfortable 70˚F (20˚C). Walking along the hallway, I have the impression of a damp, subterranean labyrinth. Meditative music mixes with the echoing drips, the water trickling down the walls to collect in small channels at the bottom, like arteries carrying the very life-blood of the mountain. Spotlights create pools of light, accentuating the tableau of stone and water.

Each room is named after a different "Alpine horizon": Sambuco, Lucendro, Rotondo, and Wilder Mann. I find myself at home in Leventina. The frugal but stylish furniture is designed by Jean. The table, bed and chairs are made from elm; the floor is larch. There is a picture on the wall above the sink which is illuminated from behind: a beautiful photograph of the sun rising behind distant peaks. I switch on the light and the picture becomes a mirror — another of Jean's bright ideas. Spring water runs from the faucets. The iron door — which weighs a mere 770 lb (350 kg)! — has a small glass slit intended to reduce the feeling of captivity. This, of course, means a reduction in privacy as well. But, if need be, the little mobile wardrobe can easily be wheeled in front of it. This is, indeed, an

ideal place to explore and perhaps redefine your personal boundaries of privacy. And not only because the luxurious bathrooms are set in a separate "wellness area" and one is likely to encounter other bathrobe-clad guests on the way there.

It soon becomes apparent that this hotel creates far more than just a pleasant atmosphere. Familiar orientation points, taken for granted in our everyday lives, are missing here. There's no distraction from the outside world through television or cell phones. Not even the sun offers its habitual rhythm in this windowless world of rock and water. Our natural sense of time and space is soon lost. And that is exactly what Jean, the sociologist, wants. He has set the stage for us to welcome and accept new experiences and new people – after all, we're all in this together. You automatically feel part of a family, an effect perhaps also due to the limited number of guests.

I soon get to know the other inhabitants of this self-contained world of stone, and the following morning I find myself feeling empathy rather than surprise as I see my neighbors crawling on all fours, busy inspecting the water channels. I join them and together we admire the clever illumination and the way it reflects in the water.

Down here in the heart of the mountain everything is different. Our isolation from everyday life not only stimulates curiosity but also sharpens the senses. There is rock, water, and light. Sparse and pure. The absence of other elements focuses the mind upon the essentials of life.

La Claustra is an oasis of revival for body and soul. It has an arcane quality, like a place from mythology. And, just like such places, it can only be reached by those prepared to explore within.

La Claustra
Raw and luxurious, meditative and communicative

● Inside a mountain, 980 ft (300 m) north of the St. Gotthard Pass, 6,725 ft (2,050 m) above sea level, within the municipality of Airolo, in the Ticino Canton of Switzerland. A 2-hr drive from Zurich or Milan.

ℹ 4-star hotel. 9 single rooms, 8 double rooms. Per person with breakfast: 215 USD (245 CHF); per person with breakfast and dinner (recommended): 285 USD (325 CHF). Open end May–end Oct.
+41 (0)91 880 5055
www.claustra.ch

Things to do

Round-table "Tavolata"
La Claustra regularly hosts entertaining and rather informative meetings called "Tavolatas". During a six-course dinner, guests enjoy fine food as well as fine conversation. Jean sends food scouts far and wide to find new culinary delights, the best ingredients and the finest wines for his hotel. He himself or one of his designated experts joins these spirited parties to reflect upon a variety of subjects. Wine Tavolatas are held in which wine connoisseurs of the region are invited to conduct a tasting. There are also Artistic Tavolatas where entertainers perform for the guests. The Tavolatas are intended to indulge the senses and

inspire the spirit – the very quintessence of La Claustra. Each Tavolata begins with a guided tour of the complex entitled "From Fortress to Oasis."

Six-course dinner, wines, guided tour through the complex, overnight stay with breakfast: 425 USD (485 CHF).

Reserve via La Claustra

Nostalgic steam train to the Ice Cave

This is a nostalgic trip in an 80-year-old steam locomotive from which you can admire the finest in Swiss railroad engineering. The train departs from the pretty mountain village of Realp and carries passengers – in beautifully renovated cars – up the mountain through several tunnels and across breathtaking bridges and stone viaducts. After stopping for water, the train reaches the station at Muttbach-Belvédère some 75 minutes later. From here, a footpath leads up to the Hotel-Restaurant Belvédère (about 40 minutes' walk), and then onto the Ice Cave at the mouth of the Rhône Glacier, situated some 7,580 ft (2,300 m) above sea level.

It's actually a man-made ice tunnel about 330 ft (100 m) long which leads up to a chamber or grotto. The purity of the water in the glacial ice gives the cave a glorious blue iridescence. Since the glacier is constantly shifting the cave has to be newly carved out every year – something that has been happening here since 1870. Be sure to wrap up warm!

Once back at the Hotel Belvédère, a Swiss postal service bus runs back to Andermatt and from there a taxi will take you back to La Claustra.

Take a taxi from La Claustra to/from Andermatt station (16 miles [26 km]; around 28 USD [32 CHF] one way). Take the local train Andermatt–Realp (15 min; 4 USD [4.80 CHF] one way; www.sbb.ch). From Realp take the Furka steam train Realp-Muttbach-Belvédère (38 USD [44 CHF] one way; departs Realp Jul–mid Aug: 10:15am & 2:15pm daily, Jun & mid-Aug–early Oct: 10:15am & 2:15pm Fri–Sun). On return take the postal service bus Belvédère–Andermatt station (around 50 min; 19 USD [21.60 CHF]; afternoon only; www.sbb.ch).
+41 (0)41 848 000 144
www.furka-bergstrecke.ch

Rhône Glacier Ice Cave: open Jun–mid-Oct: 8am–6pm (summer until 7:30pm). Cave entry: 4.50 USD (5 CHF).
+41 (0)41 279 731 129
www.gletscher.ch/grotte.html

Exploring the Göschener Valley waterways

The Waterways Trail (*Wasserweg Göschenen*) in the Göschener Valley runs through picturesque Alpine scenery along mountain streams and dams, through ravines and moorlands, past glaciers, natural springs, and Alpine lakes. Aided by the guidebook, *All About Water*, and an accompanying map you can follow a route marked by 89 points of interest showing all different facets of water. The guidebook supplies interesting information on water's role in our lives and its importance to the environment. It covers such things as why avalanches happen, how glaciers are born, and other phenomena such as floodplains, moraines (ridges caused

by glacial debris), and permafrost. Explanations are all the more amazing since the objects of their study can be examined first-hand along the way.

The trail avoids newly built roads and mainly uses old mountain paths. The special trail map helps to plan individual routes.

Trail map and guidebook: 15 USD (17 CHF) each. Order through the contact number or website below. It is also available to pick up at tourist offices in the region.
+41 (0)41 885 1834
www.wasserwelten.ch (German only)

Above (left to right): unprepossessing entrance to La Claustra; bedroom in La Claustra; interior hallway and restaurant with a Tavolata taking place; Furka steam train; Alpine lake and moorland in the Göschener Valley

21

CAPPADOCIA: TURKEY

CAVE HOTEL

CAVE HOTEL

"Using only their hands and primitive tools, the Cappadocians carved their homes deep within the soft volcanic rock creating a labyrinth of tunnels."

AS I NEAR ÜRGÜP, THE GATEWAY TO CAPPADOCIA IN TURKEY, I'm immediately enchanted by the breathtaking scenery that unfolds before my eyes. Cappadocia is a UNESCO World Heritage Site, and with good reason: it's as if I've entered a magical world of rock and stone. The forces of nature – lava, water, and wind – have sculpted a weird and wonderful lunar landscape of colossal rock chimneys in fantastic formations. The hillsides are moulded into soft rippling folds of stone. It's a natural work of art unlike anything else in the world – a surreal dreamscape.

But man has also played his part in creating this strange landscape. Many of these rock columns – lovingly referred to as "fairy chimneys" by the locals – are riddled with niches and caves so high up they seem quite inaccessible. They are, in fact, human dwellings. Using only their hands and primitive tools, the Cappadocians carved their homes deep within the soft volcanic rock creating a labyrinth of tunnels.

The area is steeped in history. Man probably first settled in Cappadocia during the Neolithic Age around 7,000 years ago, while the first cave dwellings were built over 4,000 years ago. Hittites, Phrygians, Persians, Romans, Byzantines, and Seljuks have all at one time called the fairy chimneys their home.

St. Paul first brought Christianity to Cappadocia in the early years following Christ's crucifiction. However, it wasn't until the 3rd century that Christian communities became established here. They carved churches and monasteries into the rock, with inconspicuous entrances leading to the sacred chambers. It was in these secret vaults that the early Christian monks took refuge from the marauding Arabs, and their legacy survives today: the colorful frescoes in the interiors have yellowed with age but are still awe-inspiring.

In an area so saturated with troglodyte history, what could be more appropriate than to spend some time in a cave yourself? The hotel Yunak Evleri in Ürgüp provides just that – an experience which makes visitors sense just how far we've come in the long history of our cultural development.

A cobbled side street leads up to the hotel. Did I say hotel? "Rock face" would be more appropriate: the suites and rooms lie well hidden within the caves. The upper rooms

are accessible via external steps or narrow, winding passageways through the rock.

The sense of ancient cultures, dating back many thousands of years, is ever-present. Every hollow and every rock formation seems impregnated with history. Apparently, some of the chambers in the hotel were churches in the 4th and 5th century. When you look carefully, you can still make out faint red crosses on the rock face.

There are 27 caves in total, each one bought from a local family. The characteristic crude scratch marks on the walls are evidence that these dwellings were made using a chisel. It is a centuries-old technique that required much arduous labor. Some have been used as store rooms, others as homes. Some were even pigeon lofts and you can still see the numerous pigeon holes left in the walls. The inhabitants used to farm the birds for their droppings, which were highly valued as fertilizer for the nitrate-poor volcanic soil.

Once they became part of the hotel each cave was cleaned thoroughly and had the black smoke stains scrubbed from the ceiling above the stove. My room is tastefully yet economically furnished with Turkish carpets, a sturdy metal bed, and antiques. It's fairly dark — heavy brocade curtains smother the few small windows. Even without heating, it's comfortably warm. The caves are well isolated from the cold of Cappadocian winters when the temperature can drop to -40°F (-40°C), and remain cool during the long hot summers when they climb to 95°F (35°C).

ABDULLAH INAL, GENERAL MANAGER

"You don't need to build a house in Cappadocia – the houses already exist. Stepping into these cave dwellings is like stepping over the threshold of time itself, taking you back some 2,000 years. When I greet our guests with 'Welcome home,' I mean it, literally: 'Welcome to the home of civilization itself.'"

Although you're constantly reminded of the thousands of years of history contained within these caves, staying at the hotel is a modern experience. There is a Jacuzzi in the marble bathroom, and the elegant antique cupboards are filled with mod cons, such as a stereo, television, and DVD player – so there's no chance of really getting lost in the Stone Age here.

Thinking back to our ancient ancestors and their admirable and laborious efforts building these cave dwellings, I lie back in my rocking chair and reach out to play an appropriately meditative tune on the stereo.

Yunak Evleri
Stone-Age luxury

On the outskirts of the small town of Ürgüp, close to the tourist attractions of Cappadocia, Turkey. 46 miles (75 km) from Kayseri airport, 170 miles (275 km) southeast of Ankara.

Double room: 170–245 USD (280–400 TRY) including breakfast; dinner is an additional 26 USD (43 TRY). Free internet access.
+90 (0)384 341 6920
www.yunak.com

Things to do

Hiking to the fairy chimneys

From the elevated area of what is known as Sunset Point, about 30 minutes' drive from Ürgüp, several hiking trails lead through spectacular valleys, including Güllüdere, the Rose Valley. From the path you can enjoy stunning views of the ancient and curious rock formations. It's especially beautiful in fall when the apricot trees turn orange.

By the wayside you pass a church carved into the rock. It is said that in AD 900 Christians fled here to escape the pursuing Arabs. The path leads on past the abandoned rock dwellings at Cavusin, which were still occupied up until the 1960s even though they never had running water or electricity. Finally you reach the famous Valley of the Monks (Pasabagi, also known as the Love Valley), with its remarkable fairy chimneys. The mushroom-shaped rock towers are made up of a hard weather-resistant cap and a cone-shaped base of softer stone that erodes slowly. The site is a busy tourist attraction.

Public transportation is scarce. The hotel can organize a car to take you to Sunset Point and pick you up from the Valley of the Monks. Chauffeur and car: around 60 USD (100 TRY) per day including fuel. Admission to Sunset Point (high season only): 1.80 USD (3 TRY).

Subterranean city of Kaymaklı

There are approximately 200 subterranean cities in Cappadocia, and 36 of them are open to the public. The 1.4-sq-mile (3.5-sq-km) underground metropolis of Kaymaklı was once inhabited by around 5,000 people who lived in this underground labyrinth of caves at a depth of up to 330 ft (100 m). Only the upper five levels, which descend to a depth of 115 ft (35 m), are accessible today, partly because of the possibility of a cave-in and partly due to the danger of getting lost in the maze of passages.

Important junctions were blocked for defense purposes using huge millstone-like rocks. These massive stopper stones weigh 1,100–1,320 lbs (500–600 kg) and were positioned so that they were easily rolled into place from the inside, but were unmoveable from the outside.

Apart from living quarters and places to pray, there were also subterranean stables, store rooms, toilets and washrooms, and even a wine cellar. Anyone seeking refuge here could survive for two to three months below the surface during a siege. The Byzantines hid here in the 7th century, and the Turks and the Greeks in the 13th century, while fighting the Mongols. The oldest levels of the city are around 4,000 years old.

Kaymaklı is 21 miles (35 km) from Ürgüp. Open 8:30am–7pm. Admission: 9 USD (15 TRY).

Hot-air ballooning

At dawn the voluminous hot-air balloons rise up into the morning sky, carrying their passengers in willow baskets beneath them. The view from the slowly drifting balloon is fantastic: the landscape takes on a soft pink hue in the first rays of daylight.

Only the sporadic thunderous firing of the balloon, sounding like a fire-breathing dragon breaks the morning silence. After reaching altitudes of up to 4,260 ft (1,300 m), the pilot skilfully steers the balloon to dip back into the valley, sweeping closely over the magnificent rock formations. Depending on the pilot's expertise, you might even get close enough to reach down and pluck an apple from a tree!

Many visitors make the journey to Cappadocia specifically to enjoy this breathtaking ride.

Not recommended for late risers: the ride starts with a 5am pick-up from the hotel. 1.5-hr deluxe flight (max 12 participants): 285 USD (465 TRY); 1-hr standard flight (max 21 participants): 195 USD (315 TRY).
+90 (0)384 341 5662
www.goremeballoons.com

Above (left to right): walking through the dramatic landscape on the way to the Valley of the Monks; Kaymaklı cave city; ballooning around the "fairy chimneys"

22

SABI SAND RESERVE,
SOUTH AFRICA

BED IN A TREE

"I'm alone in the wilderness, in the open. Tucked up in bed, a light breeze strokes my face and I sense how close the animals really are."

BED IN
A TREE

MY WILD BUSH ADVENTURE STARTS IN EXQUISITE LUXURY. In order to get to the bed in a tree you first have to book a room at the 5-star safari lodge, Lion Sands. My "room" turns out to be a spacious villa right on the Sabie River, with its own infinity pool, elegant black and white fittings, and impeccable service. In short, it's everything you could wish for in a 5-star hotel.

The wilds of the South African savanna, however, begin just beyond the hotel's limits. If you want to get really close, you have to book an extra bed — one right out there in the wild.

A few hours before sunset, the hotel jeep takes me out into the bush. After a bumpy, 15-minute drive along a rocky road, something white suddenly comes into view. It gleams like a distant harbor in the midst of an emerald green sea. There it is, high up in the branches of an old Leadwood tree, my bed for the night.

Steps lead us up to the wooden platform, built against a 500-year-old tree with beautiful, wild orchids growing out of its now bare and knotted boughs. An enormous four-poster bed covered with a mosquito net dominates most of the open, roofless treehouse, but there's also a small safari table and chairs, a dressing table with mirror, a valet stand complete with dressing gown, and, in the corner, an umbrella stand containing a large umbrella.

Rupert, my valet, lays the table stylishly with delicate china, silver cutlery, and ice-cold champagne. From a large safari bag he conjures up my dinner, which is no less than a sumptuously garnished six-course gourmet feast. He then shows me how to light the paraffin lamps, how to work the two-way radio (in case it rains and I want to return to the lodge), and, finally, he hands me the binoculars. They are invaluable here, with such an amazing view of the surrounding bush and all its creatures great and small. And, if I'm lucky, he says, one of the "Big Five" might pay me a visit.

So, they live down there, do they? I start to wonder. What about the ones that climb, like the leopards for which this area is so famous? Or snakes? Or anything else for that matter! "Well, to come up here would be totally against their nature," is Rupert's not altogether reassuring response. This is obviously the thrill factor that you are paying that bit extra for. I watch the jeep disappear into the green of the savanna. I'm suddenly alone. Alone with the animals, that is.

NICHOLAS MORE, CO-OWNER

"The Chalkley Treehouse was built by my grandfather who hunted in this area in the 1930s. One day, however, he found that *he* was the one being hunted – by a pair of lions. He narrowly escaped them by climbing into an old Leadwood tree. He was so grateful that he built a platform up there among the branches. In subsequent years, he took his young wife up there for Sunday picnics, but they never stayed overnight. It was my brother and I who came up with that idea."

There is certainly a lot going on down there. A huge herd of impalas graze warily while their young leap exuberantly about them. Soon to join them are herds of zebra and kudu, and a family of warthogs. The scene is one of paradise – a perfect picture of different species living harmoniously alongside one another.

Then, I do strike lucky! One of the Big Five arrives on the scene, a rhinoceros, followed by a second. A fight ensues, and the pair start to push and grunt at each other. Soon enough it cools off. Perhaps it was just a simple flexing of the muscles or a lover's tiff. It is breathtaking to watch, to spy on them from above and experience the uninhibited behavior of Africa's wild beasts. The luxury of the treehouse seems to tame the savagery of the wilderness. Still, a lion is a lion, and I doubt he would care whether I eat from a silver spoon or not.

As dusk falls upon the scene a thousand stars ignite, sparkling in a deep blue night sky. I'm alone in the wilderness, in the open. The sounds and calls of the animals are much clearer now. Tucked up in bed, a light breeze strokes my face and I sense how close the animals really are.

As I settle down for the night, I'm reminded of the old lady whose last wish was to have the once-in-a-lifetime experience of spending the night here, alone in a treetop. That night when she stayed at the treehouse it started to rain. She didn't use the radio to call for help, however. Eventually, the lodge radioed her suggesting they take her back to the dry luxury of her hotel suite. "No thank you," was her pert answer, she was "Fine. Excellent, in fact." She was lying in bed, umbrella in hand, feeling perfectly happy with the world around her – there was no reason to leave.

Chalkley & Jackalberry Treehouses
Luxury in the wild

The treehouses are located in the South African bush, a 15-min drive from the Lion Sands lodges. The resort is in a private game reserve within Sabi Sand Reserve, opposite the Kruger National Park on the other side of the Sabie River. Completely sealed off from African everyday life. 2-hr drive or 68 miles (110 km) from Nelspruit airport, 25-min drive or 7 miles (12 km) from Skukuza airport.

5-star lodge with two treehouses available, to be booked in addition to a room at the lodge. Tip: Chalkley Treehouse, the original (mentioned in the text), has a better view while Jackalberry has a leafy canopy.

There is no running water at the treehouses. Chemical toilets and wash bowls are on the landing below the platform. It is advisable to come out several hours before dark to have enough time to watch the animals. Pick up the next morning as per arrangement or ad hoc via radio. Malaria prophylaxis is essential.

Lion Sands lodges: double room from 935 USD (8,300 ZAR); suite from 1,650 USD (14,700 ZAR). The bed in a tree costs an additional 135 USD (1,185 ZAR). Reduced prices in low season (May–Sep).

+27 (0)11 484 9911
www.lionsands.com

Things to do

Bush Walk
A morning excursion on foot. This is a leisurely safari paying special attention to the smaller animals and plants of the African bush. It includes an introduction to the medicinal properties of the plants and to the tracking of animals.
No extra cost for hotel guests.

Classic Safari
This is a professionally run safari trip in a huge open-topped Land Rover. The tracker sits on a specially constructed seat on the front of the vehicle from where he tracks the animals. The Sabi Sand Reserve is famous for its leopards, but also for the rest of the Big Five: elephants, rhino, buffalo, and lions.
No extra cost for hotel guests.

Astronomer's Safari
A different take on the traditional safari: during an evening game drive, away from the lights of the lodge, guests lie back and are taken on a journey through the southern night sky. Not only for those interested in the solar system, the safari also covers the African myths and legends associated with the stars.
No extra cost for hotel guests.
Reserve all safaris via Lion Sands

Above (left to right): Ivory Lodge suite at Lion Sands; leopard; hotel guests on a Bush Walk; trailing a leopard on a Classic Safari

ELEPHANT
TENT

23

ADDO NATIONAL PARK:
SOUTH AFRICA

ELEPHANT TENT

"We spot the culprit of this early morning disturbance: an enormous bull elephant is having a scratch. It is a majestic and truly impressive sight."

I'M WOKEN IN THE EARLY HOURS OF THE MORNING BY PECULIAR SCUFFING NOISES, and the whole house is shaking. Is it an earthquake? No, I suddenly remember that I'm actually in a tent and that the hotel staff had warned me not to panic if this sort of thing happened. At the Addo National Park such occurrences can generally be ascribed to the park's most eminent inhabitants – the elephants.

Carefully, I take a peek outside and catch a glimpse of ... my neighbors doing the same. We exchange nervous grins and take a few wary steps forward, purposely staying close to the supposed safety of our tented bungalows.

The scuffing noises have now developed into the loud cracking sound of tree branches being broken. We spot the culprit of this early morning disturbance: an enormous bull elephant is having a scratch. It is a majestic and truly impressive sight. Our reverential whispers of admiration turn into a communal sigh of relief as he sedately disappears into the bush.

Unlike other game reserves in South Africa, the Gorah Elephant Camp doesn't use fences. The animals are left free to roam at will, even right up to the bungalows. Although an encounter as close as this is

201

NICOLA SCHWIM

"I believe there is a special connection between the elephants and Gorah Camp. Their ancient spirit protects us. By the light of the full moon, the elephants gather around the house and trumpet their song. The tale of Gorah farm is like that of the elephants – one of the matriarch. The farm has always been governed by women, in the same way that herds of elephants are always led by a female."

not an everyday occurrence, sooner or later everybody is likely to see one – the Addo National Park has the highest density of elephants on earth.

I return to my bungalow, which feels more like a tent than a house, although a very robust tent with a wooden floor and roof. It gives you a feeling of safety, offering protection from the elephants and other beasts, and indeed nothing untoward has ever happened here. The walls are made of canvas giving the room a light and airy safari quality. There is also a touch of colonial luxury with a four-poster bed in rich dark wood, silver trays of exotic nuts, and elegant chairs offering a veranda view of the expansive African savanna. It's like something from *Out of Africa*. You can easily imagine a delicate English lady seated at her davenport desk composing passionate letters to England.

Throughout the hotel there is little modern technology to spoil the nostalgic atmosphere. Apart from a small solar energy plant to power the ventilators and a few lights, Gorah is electricity-free. This distinguishes it further from other safari lodges. Candles and paraffin lamps replace light bulbs; the pervasive odor of the paraffin is something you have to get used to. Heating and cooking is done by gas, and meals are taken in the main lodge.

Our breakfast is served on the veranda overlooking the waterhole just 100 ft (30 m) away. In the mornings, ostrich, which were once bred here for their feathers, can be seen drinking at the waterhole where they are joined by zebra and kudu. This is a place of harmonious co-existence of man and beast at breakfast. Cheeky warthogs venture closer to the lodge bending at the knee in a dainty little bow to chew the

grass. Next door, the big communal veranda provides soft couches and a telescope for a closer look at the action.

The jovial voices of the kitchen staff carry over to us. Don't miss the opportunity to ask William to tell the story of the flightless dung beetle in his native African language. The curious sequence of precise clicking sounds made with the tongue and throat seem sheer feats of acrobatic proportion to Western ears.

There's an exceptionally friendly community spirit among the staff. In the evening, dinner is served by romantic candlelight, and the white rangers, who lead the guests on safari during the day, help their black colleagues serve what the African bush has to offer – crocodile, impala, kudu, and ostrich.

At the end of the evening, to avoid any closer encounter with the African wildlife (other than "well done" on our plates), the rangers escort us along boardwalks safely back to our tents. Then we are alone, with only the flimsy canvas between us and the elephants of Africa.

Gorah Elephant Camp
"Out of Africa" in a tent

In the middle of Addo National Park, East Cape, South Africa. About 40 miles (65 km) or a 1-hr drive from Port Elizabeth.

5-star hotel with swimming pool. Modern bathrooms are in the rear of the tents.

This central sector of the Addo National Park is home to 450 elephants, 300 buffalo, 14 black rhinoceroses, 9 lions, 180 eland, 2,000 kudu, innumerable warthogs, ostrich, wildebeest, bushbucks, jackals, hyenas, and some 300 species of bird.

There are 11 tents. Tent including all meals and safari game drives: Apr–Sep 310 USD (2,750 ZAR); Sep–Dec 630 USD (5,595 ZAR); Jan–Apr 675 USD (5,990 ZAR).
+ 27 (0)44 501 1111
www.hunterhotels.com/gorahelephantcamp

Things to do

Gorah Camp safaris

Hotel guests generally take part in safaris twice daily, once at 8:30am and again at 4:30pm. These are definitely the highlight of any visit to the park. Riding in open jeeps, rangers drive guests into the bush for a closer look at Africa's wildlife. No two trips are the same: the diversity of species and their random behavior seem inexhaustible.

The safaris at Gorah distinguish themselves by their exceptionally knowledgeable guides. This is far more than a mere photo opportunity. The enthusiasm of the young rangers is contagious and soon has everyone excited. Our guide, Johan, points out the smaller, often unnoticed inhabitants of the bush, a termite mound for instance, or the endemic flightless dung beetle. Their larger cohabitants are also present and the possibility of seeing a lion or a black rhino is very high.

Observing the social behavior of these animals is fascinating. We see the servile demeanor of the lion cub when playing with his father, and then his impudence when marking right over his father's territory once the adult has departed. No less memorable is an encounter with the largest and most imposing of all animals: the elephant. A charging bull elephant is certainly overwhelming, and it's a good thing to have an experienced guide along. As dusk gathers, Johan produces a table and we sit and relive the events of the day over canapés and a cool glass of wine.
Reserve via Gorah Elephant Camp

Above (left to right): lions overlooking Addo National Park; a Gorah Camp safari with zebra and kudu; elephants grazing in the Camp

24

SOUTH ARI ATOLL:
MALDIVES

GLASS-FLOOR VILLA

GLASS-FLOOR
VILLA

"The most enthralling feature of this ultra-luxurious abode has to be the living area's glass floor, below which swarms of needlefish can be seen swimming happily beneath us, heedless of our presence."

THE MALDIVES ARE THE ULTIMATE DREAM DESTINATION FOR SUN worshippers and scuba divers alike. Over 1,100 coral islets form this island nation. Grouped into 26 atolls, they have evolved from oceanic volcanoes — as the interiors of the volcanoes have gradually subsided they have left a fringe of growing coral reef in a ring around an open center, which forms a lagoon. From our plane the islets look like a string of pearls embedded in rich deep-blue cobalt. None rise more than 8 ft (2.5 m) above sea level, making the Maldives the flattest nation in the world.

After landing on an airport island near Malé, we transfer to a tiny, bright-red seaplane which is to carry us on to our hotel — although we have to wait for two hours for it to fill up with enough passengers. After a 30-minute flight southwest we finally catch a glimpse of the Conrad hotel islands, Rangali and Rangalifinolhu. A footbridge that connects the two islands shimmers between them like a long silvery thread. We land directly on the water in the middle of the bright turquoise lagoon, which makes a wonderfully wide and soft landing strip.

The friendly hotel staff welcome us with 5-star smiles and remind us of the one-hour time difference with Malé, now 55 miles (90 km) away. Yes, the Conrad hotel has its very own time zone, which supposedly gives its guests an extra hour in the evening and allows them a luxurious lie-in in the morning! The hotel offers several restaurants (in "barefoot-luxury" style), two spas, baby sharks basking in the shallows of immaculate white beaches, and, in the gathering dusk, fruit bats that flap between the islands like ungainly birds.

The resort has a pleasant and professional ambience and 5- or even 6-star comfort according to the hotel's own categorization. This doesn't, however, make the islands feel ostentatious — on the contrary, they seem rather natural and unpretentious. Perhaps this is because of the size of the resort, as it is, at least by Maldivian standards, quite large: the distance is 2 miles (3 km) from one end of the islands to the other. Or maybe it's because they offer three different categories of luxury, true to the hotel's slogan: "One resort, two islands, three luxurious experiences." However, it's still more than likely that even the guests staying in their standard accommodation have traveled here by business class, at least.

Well, ours must be the "super-deluxe-extra-platinum" category. A specially appointed speedboat takes us out to our Sunset Water Villa, which actually at first glance looks like a rather unspectacular wooden hut on stilts. Two such sun-bleached villas stand nobly apart from the rest. Of course, we also have our own dedicated footbridge (should we want to walk) stretching 100 ft (30 m) back to the white sandy beach. A young man in a bright-green outfit turns out to be our personal butler. At the push of a button he will glide inconspicuously in and out through a separate entrance, attending to our every whim.

"Villa" is no understatement. Here, big is, indeed, beautiful. In this bright and illustrious island paradise, money not only buys you time, it buys you space. Spread over some 660 sq ft (200 sq m), our suite has just about everything you could possibly wish for — and much more. Light pours in through panoramic windows, and glass doors allow for spectacular views across the bright-turquoise lagoon. The villa feels spacious, open, and airy. There are no walls separating the bedroom from the bathroom and the living room. All is one huge open space. But the most enthralling feature of this ultra-

CARSTEN SCHIECK, GENERAL MANAGER

"We wanted to go that one step further and offer something genuinely unique, something that no other hotel could offer. Innovation has played a big part in creating this resort. Now you can get close to the spectacular world of Maldivian marine life without even getting your feet wet."

luxurious abode has to be the living area's enormous glass floor, below which swarms of needlefish can be seen swimming happily beneath us, heedless of our presence. We're immediately tempted to pull away the armchairs, which appear to be floating on the water itself, and stretch out on the glass to watch the multitudes of fish. Only we don't because other highlights grab our attention.

Everything here is exclusive. Nothing is mediocre — there is high-tech audio equipment from Bose, a marble bathroom well stocked with Philippe Stark and Bulgari products, a big Jacuzzi with an impressive control pad, and another Jacuzzi out on the veranda. A telescope is conveniently positioned behind the panoramic windows to zoom in on the 6-star view. And then there's the bed — big, round, and decorated with little orange flowers. At the touch of a button, this sumptuous divan is designed to rotate very slowly, following the path of the setting sun.

All this spectacular luxury proves rather demanding! Before pampering ourselves to oblivion, we have to decipher the remote controls. Even our attempts at simply switching the light on remain unsuccessful. And then it suddenly occurs to me — I have only to press that one special button and our butler will do the rest!

So, what do we do now — watch the fish perform beneath the living room floor, or wait until the show really gets going in the evening, when the lights of the villa attract even larger swarms of nosy fish? Perhaps in the meantime I'll have a bath. But which Jacuzzi shall I choose — the posh marble one or the smaller one on the sundeck? This is a problem even the butler can't solve. This is definitely not a place for the indecisive, but I've made my choice — I pick the largest pool of all and dive head-first into the shimmering turquoise of the Indian Ocean.

Sunset Water Villas
Exquisite. Exclusive. Expensive.

Conrad Maldives Rangali, Rangali and Rangalifinolhu Islands, South Ari Atoll, the Maldives.

The resort can be reached only by seaplane from Malé (flight time about 30 min). Transfer by Maldivian Air Taxi: 400 USD. It is important to arrive before the last shuttle flight at 6pm to avoid having to spend a night in Malé (there are no night flights).

Sunset Water Villa for up to 4 people: from 5,500 USD in low season to 8,000 USD in peak season.
+960 668 0629
www.conradhotels.com

Things to do

Swimming with manta rays

This is an absolute must for anybody who is able to scuba dive. Ten minutes by boat from the hotel and located on the Madivaru Reef is Manta Point, a place regularly visited by the mighty manta ray. These majestic animals usually live 660–1000 ft (200–300 m) below the surface, but between December and April they swim up to the reef to let the helpful cleaner-wrasse fish free their skin of parasites. The water is about 45 ft (14 m) deep here and offers the opportunity for an unforgettable encounter with these gentle but imposing giants whose wing span can measure up to 25 ft (7 m).

Also suitable for inexperienced divers.

1-hr dive including equipment and guide: 80 USD.
Reserve via Conrad Maldives Rangali

Dining above the waves

For those who would like to visit one of the typically tiny islets of the Maldives, the island paradise of Baros is highly recommended. Here, you can dine above the waves, at the height of a palm tree – the highest you'll get in the Maldives. The two-storey Lighthouse Restaurant is built upon stilts in the ocean, surrounded by glorious turquoise waters. Enjoy a cocktail in the top-story lounge from where you can gaze out across the atoll with its shimmering lagoon and marvel at the intense play of different shades of blue. In the restaurant you are seated directly next to the water. It's the perfect spot to enjoy a romantic sunset as stingrays swim by, the trusty sommelier at your side.

A speedboat collects guests from Malé (20 min). Reservation required. Lighthouse Restaurant of 5-star hotel Baros. Three-course meal with half a bottle of wine: around 120 USD.
+960 664 2672
www.baros.com

Dining beneath the waves

This truly unique experience takes place on the seabed itself. Fifteen feet (5 m) below the surface of the Indian Ocean, the Conrad Rangali team serves fine food and wines. In a transparent acrylic tunnel, diners have a near all-round view of the fish passing by or overhead. At this depth there is a greater variety and number of fish to be seen than when snorkeling. The stingrays soar over the diners' heads, attracted by regular afternoon feedings that ensure their appearance. Feast your eyes on the fascinating and colorful underwater world of the Maldives while feasting your palate on the culinary delights of the hotel's kitchen.

This is the only underwater restaurant in the world with a completely transparent ceiling. It seats 12. Smart dress and a reservation well in advance are required.

Five-course West Maldivian Culinary-Fusion dinner: 320 USD.
Reserve via Conrad Maldives Rangali

Above (left to right): manta ray; upper and lower deck of the Lighthouse Restaurant; a stingray gliding past a table at the Conrad Maldives Rangali underwater restaurant

215

THROAT OF
A TROLL

25

THROAT OF
A TROLL

"A passageway, dimly
lit with electric
torches, winds
downward. At the
bottom it suddenly
broadens into a cozy
cave-like chamber
where pink and
green lights play on
the walls."

A TROLL PEERS AT ME, HIS EYES SHINING IN THE TWILIGHT. His mouth – like the rest of him built out of stone – is held patiently agape as if waiting to gobble up the unwary newcomer. He is not intimidating, however – it is far too peaceful here. The evening sun touches the eucalyptus trees while two horses graze beside a lake in the valley below. A car, elaborately painted with dragons and fairies, creaks to a halt beside me and an attractive couple step out: he, lean with graying temples and an intelligent face; she, slender with warm eyes and a boyish hair cut. They are Nobby and Sheila Ward, the visionaries who created Mira Mira.

Mira Mira is the Aboriginal spelling of "Mirror, mirror." "... on the wall, whose is the craziest hotel of all?" adds Nobby. The name came to him on a particularly windless afternoon. "The lake was perfectly calm and I could see the troll's three terraces clearly reflected in its surface – just like in a mirror," he explains. "Three terraces...?" I wonder, but Nobby has already pulled open the wooden door that is the troll's mouth, and disappeared into the darkness of its throat.

A passageway, dimly lit with electric torches, winds downward. At the bottom it

NOBBY WARD, CREATOR AND CO-BUILDER

"I found out a while ago that I am terminally ill with cancer. But that wasn't the end. In fact, it was a beginning. It gave me the motivation to finally do the things I've always wanted to do. That's how Mira Mira came about. It sounds strange, but first I had to find out I was dying, before I could really start living."

suddenly broadens into a cozy cave-like chamber where pink and green lights play on the walls, illuminating the stalactites and stalagmites that divide the room in half. The sound of dripping water echoes softly in the background, just like in a real cave. Only this one is equipped with a modern kitchen complete with microwave, a dining area, a couch, a fireplace, and, yes, here it is – even a large terrace! That's why it's pleasantly light down here. The terrace is set up with garden furniture, a barbecue and a glorious view of the shimmering lake below. You can also see the imposing Reception Center with its towers and dragon figures and the gently rolling hills beyond. What a perfect place to spend a lazy summer's evening.

When Nobby planned the position of The Cave House, Mother Nature was an important consideration: the hot sun of the Australian summer doesn't shine far into the rooms, so when the heat rages outside, the cave stays cool and pleasant. In winter, the rays of the low-lying sun reach deep into the rooms, warming them naturally. Ecologically friendly architecture is one of Nobby's major concerns.

The first of the two bedrooms is a round chamber, also with its own terrace. Facing the terrace, an oval recess in the cave wall hides a double bed, stuffed with gaudy, fluffy pillows. "I wanted to evoke a feeling of utter safety in there," says Nobby, "like that of a baby in its mother's womb. I wanted to draw on the collective subconscious and our primeval instincts."

Well, that sounds like an excellent concept for a good night's sleep. I tentatively lie back on the bed and gaze out from my little cave-within-a-cave. The chamber's ceiling is covered with fairy lights, creating the illusion of a star-studded sky. The baby and the universe.... This is where micro- and macrocosm come together.

Nobby truly has put a huge amount of thought into the The Cave House. Unbelievably, he and Sheila built it entirely by themselves. Nobby provided the original designs, into which he has incorporated his "philosophy of the primeval" as much as possible, although it is often tongue-in-cheek. Sheila's part was to make it cozy and give it that finishing touch: she decorated the walls with ferns and shells and other elements inspired by prehistoric times, turning it into a caveman's dream.

Inspiration is found at every turn, and not only in the field of theoretical philosophy. The second bedroom appeals to another basic instinct: lust. The room is dominated by a large four-poster bed, which looks out onto the third terrace. The leather straps and horse harnesses that hang from the frame have inspired many who have stayed here. "It wasn't exactly planned," says Sheila, "but obviously the room fulfils a certain need. We were surprised when people called to book 'The Bondage Room.'" Enthusiastic entries in the guest book give testimony to its success: "You've added new spice to my marriage," somebody claims happily.

Nobby and Sheila don't mind. Nobby, in fact, always had a certain provocative inclination, and since finding out he has cancer this has increased considerably. Nowadays, he likes to get straight to the point so as to avoid wasting valuable time.

To stay at Mira Mira is inspiring. Perhaps it's because Nobby and Sheila's positive and optimistic vitality rub off on everyone they meet. Or it's because of the relaxed atmosphere of these beautiful surroundings, or the feeling of security that radiates from the cave. Or maybe it's simply a subtle mixture of it all. Mira Mira infects you with a hunger for adventure. It makes you feel you want to get up and grasp whatever it is you want from life. Mira Mira is the beginning of the rest of your life.

The Cave House
Peaceful. Protective. And perfectly private

Mira Mira, Neerim South, Victoria, Australia. Located in the hilly bushland close to Neerim South, around a 1.5-hr drive from Melbourne. A large metal dragon is entwined around the grand entry gate.

The Cave House has two double rooms. Price per couple for 2-night minimum stay including breakfast: weekend 355 USD (490 AUD); weekday 285 USD (390 AUD).

Alongside The Cave House, Mira Mira also offers further unusual accommodations: the Japanese Zen Retreat and Tanglewood, all built by Nobby and Sheila.
+61 (0)3 5626 72000
www.miramira.com.au

Things to do

Toorongo Waterfalls
This is a lovely day trip and, in Australian terms, only just around the corner 30 miles (47 km) north of Neerim South. A shady footpath leads from the Toorongo Falls parking lot alongside the river to an observation deck at the foot of the falls. The grassy areas near the end of the footpath are great for picnics.

On the way there, visit Trestle Bridge near Noojee, an impressive wooden railroad bridge built in 1919 almost entirely by hand. With luck you may arrive in time for the Long Lunch event, which usually takes place in March. This is when tables are set up along the entire length of the bridge and diners enjoy a lunch with a view.
www.visitvictoria.com

The Animal Hospital
Get a look behind the scenes of one of Australia's zoos. The Animal Hospital at Healesville Sanctuary offers visitors a unique chance to follow the work of their surgeons as they operate. A large observation window allows you to follow the action, and the vets will even open the operating room door to answer questions while they work. The operating room is fitted with cameras, which transmit live pictures onto two large monitors in the visitors' room.

Almost all of the animal patients are brought here by local residents, which in Australian terms can mean from up to 60 miles (100 km) away. Traffic accidents account for the highest proportion of injuries – an average of 100 animals a month are treated for injuries sustained on roads alone. The hospital also conducts research in cooperation with the University of Victoria: detailed post-mortems are carried out on each deceased animal to help develop preventive medicine. They also rear endangered species such as several types of wallaby and Tasmanian Devil, ultimately releasing them back into the wild.

Healesville Sanctuary is quite a small zoo and not comparable with a typical American zoo. The main attraction is the Animal Hospital.

The road from Mira Mira to Healesville runs through the beautiful Latrobe Forest with its eucalyptus trees – a nice spot to stop for a walk.

Healesville Sanctuary is north of Melbourne, around 50 miles (80 km) from Neerim South. Admission: 17 USD (23.60 AUD).
+61 (0)3 5957 2800
www.zoo.org.au

Hidden Secrets shopping tour, Melbourne
Go shopping in the fashion capital of Australia on a guided tour with a difference. Learn tips and tricks on finding the hidden, but oh-so-desirable, boutiques and specialist stores that even the Melburnians don't know about.

Special emphasis is put on local fashion and young designers, but visits to a traditional confectioner, an enormous second-hand store, and a historic arcade, all add much appreciated variety to the tour. This is no endless string of changing rooms but a mission of discovery, with more than 50 stores to visit. The tour ends with lunch, after which you are at liberty to hurry back to those particularly enticing boutiques to peruse at will.

The tour is highly entertaining and gives a wealth of little details and anecdotes on Melbourne's lanes and arcades, as well as numerous facts on architecture. Quite obviously, it's dominated by women.

"Lanes and Arcades Tour": 10am–1:30pm Tue–Sat. Melbourne is 65 miles (100 km) from Neerim South. Tour including lunch and a "shopping bag" with information and a street map: 84 USD (115 AUD).
+61 (0)3 9329 9665, cell +61 (0)418 332 027 (reservation by text message is possible)
www.hiddensecretstours.com

Above (left to right): lake and valley view on the approach to The Cave House, Mira Mira; Toorongo Waterfalls; lace monitor being treated at Healesville Sanctuary Animal Hospital; historic Royal Arcade, Melbourne

26

WAITOMO:
NEW ZEALAND

IN A PLANE

"With one foot on the Bristol's pedal, my hands on the round steering column, and the horizon in front of us, I really feel we could take off at any second."

PLANE MOTEL
GUESTS ONLY
www.waitomomotel.co.nz

DRIVING ALONG A LITTLE SIDE ROAD in New Zealand's fairy-tale mountain landscape near the famous Waitomo Caves I catch a glimpse of a large airplane in a field. Am I dreaming? No, it really is a plane, painted in army camouflage colors and hidden behind a herd of black bulls. It belongs to Woodlyn Park whose attractions are heralded by a series of rather unsubtle signs along the roadside, advertising, "Billy Black's Kiwi Culture Show" and "unique accommodation."

And unique it is. These days you don't come across a 1940s Bristol B-170 Freighter plane very often. In fact, most people will never get the chance to see one – let alone sleep in one. There isn't a single aircraft of this type remaining in service. The only other model in the country that is accessible to the public can be admired at the Royal New Zealand Air Force Museum in Christchurch. Happily, here at Waitomo you can spend the night in one!

Up close, the plane is even larger than it looked from a distance. Underneath one of its sheltering wings is a picnic table. Birds flit about in the propellers. Inside, two vacation units have been created: one in the back of the plane, the other in the cockpit. Just when I'm trying to figure out how to work the hidden door handle along comes a sporty man in a wool T-shirt who seems delighted to be of service. It's Barry Woods, alias Billy Black, Woodlyn Park's owner. He is in his early 50s and his first gray hair is beginning to show. He is very helpful, even a bit shy, really nothing like those shrill ads suggest. He shows me how the door handle to the former cargo bay pulls down – of course, a protruding door handle is not very aerodynamic. Barry deliberately kept it exactly as it was – he just loves it when guests have to figure things out for themselves. He shows me a repaired hole in the outside wall where a bullet had whizzed through, right between a highly explosive load and the crew. The plane carried military freight and personnel into Thailand and Hong Kong and apparently was one of the last Allied planes deployed in the Vietnam War.

Inside at first nothing hints at the plane's eventful history. The bare metal walls have been plastered and painted white and blue. The rear unit holds a small kitchen, a bunk bed, a double bed, and plastic chairs. It is furnished simply, but is clean and well-suited for a couple or a family. The cozy tapered berth with its double bed and small rounded windows gives more of an "airplane" feeling.

Things are different in the cockpit unit. In the front of the plane there's a living room area where narrow steps lead up to the flight deck. Barry has trouble squeezing through the narrow opening. Here the air of fate blows strongly. You can feel it in the ripped seats, the round rudder control, the dangling cables, and, literally, through the ill-fitting windows. Up front there's a fascinating array of black and red dials, levers, switches, and knobs that can still be moved and twiddled. This is a machine-lover's paradise, the kind that small (and large) boys dream of. Some of the buttons have alarming labels such as "Emergency Fire Extinguisher" and "Operating Limitations" – not too comforting, but at least authentic.

The planes's two Bristol Hercules 14-cylinder radial engines have a capacity of 2,030 horsepower each. They would use 120 gallons (530 liters) of fuel each hour, Barry tells me, as well as large quantities of oil. We clamber into the pilot seats. With one foot on the Bristol's pedal, my hands on the round steering column (which still moves up and down smoothly), and the horizon in front of us, I really feel we could take off at any second to some faraway country.

I think of the men who once sat here carrying out less romantic missions and I can only feel sorry for them. They were exposed to grave dangers on questionable orders, above all the order not to think for

BARRY WOODS, OWNER

"I have always wanted to be number one. It was the same in my sheep shearing days. Along with a few others I still hold a world record in speed shearing. I have toured the world as a professional sheep shearer and seen many countries, and I suppose that is why I feel I know what people want in terms of entertainment and tourism. Now I want to be number one with my accommodation. My goal is to offer the most unconventional accommodation in the entire world."

themselves. Today, thank goodness, those times are gone and we can let our fantasies run free. Like Barry.

Barry's eyes sparkle as he describes his favorite hobby of playing tricks on friends and visitors. He has devised something special for naughty boys. There is a red lever in the cockpit which is strictly forbidden. When the inevitable happens and a cheeky boy ignores his parents' warnings and shifts the lever the sound of a loud engine revving up can suddenly be heard. It's startlingly realistic. This is typical of Barry's Kiwi humor, and is guaranteed to be a winner with parents.

Immediately behind the cockpit a double bed has been squeezed in. It's not ideal for claustrophobics since the ceiling is so low you can barely sit upright. I pick up the guest book as a bedtime read. Amazingly, it contains entries made by former pilots of this very aircraft! It soon transports me to a realm of airplanes and pilots — the powerful smell of machinery doing the rest. It's no wonder the men felt the need for poetics to

sweeten the load, like the longing words written on the fuselage: "Arise my Love and come with me." After a long, final look at the stars twinkling in the sky, I lie back and hope for pleasant dreams — preferably of flying.

The Plane Motel
For machine-lovers. Ideal for families

Woodlyn Park, Waitomo, North Island, New Zealand. Situated in a fairy-tale landscape of gently rolling hills not too far from the film location of Middle Earth, home of the Hobbits in *The Lord of the Rings.* It is 0.3 miles (0.5 km) from Waitomo Village, which has a store, a restaurant, and a visitors' center with a cave museum.

Rear unit (double bed closed off by a curtain and bunk beds in the living room): 85 USD (150 NZD); cockpit unit (double bed closed off by a curtain, a steep stairway leading up to a second double bed in front of the original controls): 95 USD (160 NZD).

Barry offers other unusual accommodations in Woodlyn Park, including a decommissioned train wagon, a Hobbit Motel, and, the latest addition, an original World War II patrol boat.
+64 (0)7 878 6666
www.woodlynpark.co.nz

Things to do

Billy Black's Kiwi Culture Show

Run by Barry, this humorous show will entertain young and old alike. The audience learns about New Zealand's pioneer history while watching and participating in a farm show. Among the stars of the performance are his white donkey, Donk, the black pig, Trevor, a New Zealand opossum (the "Kiwi Bear"), and, of course, plenty of sheep.

Daily show 1:30 pm: 13 USD (23 NZD).
Reserve via Woodlyn Park

Glowworm caves

This must-see cave tour starts with a visit to a dry stalactite cave where you can view fossils of New Zealand's extinct bird, the flightless Moa. The real highlight, however, is without doubt the visit to the glowworm caves.

Equipped with helmets and lights, the group (maximum 12) walks several feet in the dark before reaching a landing stage to an underground lake and a rubber dingy. The guide entertainingly explains the bizarre life-cycle of the glowworms. New Zealand glowworms are not beetles like the "fireflies," or *Lampyridae*, found in Europe. They are actually the larvae of a type of gnat. The larvae live for up to a year in darkness before pupating and emerging as mouthless, adult flies to spend a few precious days reproducing before dying. Their greenish light is a lure to attract insects, which they then ensnare and devour.

It is an unforgettable, magical experience to glide silently along the river in the dark contemplating the thousands and thousands of dots of glowworm light gleaming on the cave's ceiling. They illuminate the river, which stretches out before the boat like the glowing light of a far-off galaxy. For a coffee break with a difference ask to have your tea and coffee served inside the cave!

Spellbound Tours, Waitomo Village. 3.5-hr cave tour: 38 USD (65 NZD).
+64 (0)7 878 7621, or toll-free within New Zealand: 0800 773 552
www.glowworm.co.nz

Thermal hot-water pools of Kawhia

Hidden in the sleepy harbor town of Kawhia is a rare natural gem. At the end of a little beach path, right in the black sand, you can find thermal hot pools. They are (as yet) known only to a few, and are still not signposted. To help tourists locate the pools the information center in the town's harbor museum provides free maps. You will have to dig your own pool, but you can borrow a shovel from Annie's Café & Restaurant opposite the harbor.

To make the most of the experience ensure you arrive 30 minutes before low tide to create your own hot-water pool. Only about an hour later the pools will be flooded with seawater again. To find the springs look out for hot water steaming or bubbling up out of the sand and a smell of sulfur. Once found, scoop out a deep hole in the black sand and pile up a little edge around it to create a pool filled with lovely warm water.

This natural phenomenon is a result of geothermal activity caused by the movement of the two tectonic plates that New Zealand straddles. The result is a bathtub heated by Mother Nature herself with a guaranteed ocean view!

Kawhia Hot Water Beach is located 21 miles (35 km) or a 1.5-hr drive along winding roads from Waitomo. On reaching Kawhia, ask for directions to the beach road. Drive to the very end, about 2.5 miles (4 km), where there is a parking lot and restrooms. The hot pools are found just over the sand dune.
www.nzhotpools.co.nz

Learn to surf in Raglan

Raglan is New Zealand's unsurpassed surfing mecca – even the professionals surf here. With the Raglan Surfing School you can learn how to master the waves. A 3-hour lesson begins with practical theory and a few dry runs on the beautifully glittering black sand of the beach before heading into the water. Nearly everyone manages to get up onto the surfboard and glide with the waves toward the beach, keeping their cool at least for a few seconds. But beware: you might become addicted after just one try and, from that moment on, feel the call of the waves forever!

Raglan is about a 2-hr drive from Waitomo on the main road. Note that if you take the detour via Kawhia (see above) it's about a 4-hr drive on a partially unpaved road. Raglan Surfing School 3-hr group lesson (5 max) for beginners including wetsuit, surfboard, and a sauna afterwards: 52 USD (89 NZD); 3-hr private lesson for advanced surfers including wetsuit, surfboard, and a sauna: 75 USD (129 NZD); half a day's surfboard and wetsuit rental only, available directly on the beach: 26 USD (45 NZD).
+64 (0)7 825 7873
www.raglansurfingschool.co.nz

Above (left to right): the rolling hills of Waitomo; sheep shearing demonstration at Woodlyn Park; the magical glowworm caves; digging a thermal bath on Kawhia beach; learning to surf in Raglan

27

KAIKOURA
NEW ZEALAND

TREEHOUSES

"The view is fantastic – a large panoramic window provides a vista of the majestic Kaikoura Mountains. From the windows on the other side, I can see the sparkling blue ocean."

there is a rather extraordinary sight to behold. Five huge wooden boxes on thin stilts are towering in the tops of the native Manuka trees. I can't help but think of *Star Wars* and the Imperial Army's AT-AT walkers that always seemed to collapse under their top-heavy load. Well, these are the treehouses where I'll be spending the night. As I near the huge constructions, however, I'm reassured – their stilts are made of solid steel.

First, I head to reception. In Hapuku Lodge the prevailing ambience is one of warm friendliness coupled with an unintrusive professionalism. The exquisite furnishings and elegant designs add a sense of luxury. In all, it makes the perfect mix for the ultimate relaxation getaway – and all in a treehouse!

Tony Wilson, who co-owns and co-founded the lodge with his brother, greets me at reception. Tony is a wiry man in his early 60s with a charming, calm, and direct manner. He escorts me to my treehouse, Tui, named after the New Zealand songbird with its loud, distinctive call. Mine is the fourth in a row of five treetop rooms, all of which are named after native New Zealand birds. The imposing treehouses stand in a grove of Manuka trees, the miraculous trees whose blossom is the source for antibiotic honey and the base for countless alternative medicines. A faint hint of the wonderful sweet scent wafts from the trees.

A sturdy staircase leads upward. It has a wall made from a screen of branches and thick twigs. In fact, up here I'm surrounded by branches – we're 33 ft (10 m) above ground and level with the treetops.

The treehouse consists of one large room that is spacious and pleasantly airy. The view is fantastic – a large panoramic window provides a vista of the majestic Kaikoura Mountains, which rise to a height of 8,560 ft (2,610 m). Snow covers the peaks like powdered sugar for nearly half the year. From the windows on the other side I can see the sparkling blue ocean. Below the treehouse, a group of grazing deer is a reminder of how, back in the mid-1990s, the lodge began its life as a deer farm. The Wilsons still raise top-quality deer and also sell the velvet antler for its medicinal uses.

The room is elegant and captivating in its stylish simplicity. Many of the pieces of furniture are unique items that Tony and his brother, Michael, designed and had built right here in the on-site workshop.

Elements such as the natural shape of the Californian Redwood bark used for the bed-head, or the fine grain of Brazilian Lacewood, have been cleverly integrated into the design, giving the room the appropriately natural look it deserves. But there's even a touch of Ikea, too – the lamps and chairs in front of the cast-iron stove can probably be found anywhere in the world. This doesn't interfere with the overall sense of exclusivity, however. In fact, the mix creates a charmingly unpretentious and cozy scene.

Everything a pampered guest could wish for is here: a Jacuzzi with carefully polished jets and buttons, a DVD-player and flat-screen TV, a Bose stereo system with iPod, and WLan for those who can't live without the internet. There is also blissful under-floor heating, the fluffiest towels, and a light blanket made of silky soft possum hair – for that extra bit of sensual indulgence.

Absolute comfort is the most important thing for Tony – only the very best will do for him. He has an ever-watchful eye for detail, as much for a loose lightbulb as for the selection of choice materials used to

TONY WILSON, CO-OWNER

"When we were children, my brother and I had a kind of tree fort. It was pretty rudimentary but fantastically high up in a tree and close to the birds. We built our treehouses to remind us of this childhood experience. However, at the same time, we made sure that the new treehouses had all the luxury and comfort that we have earned as adults. Our goal was to build accommodation offering all the comforts that we ourselves wish for when we travel."

furnish the lodge. He was particularly concerned with the quality of the beds, and literally traveled the world looking for the perfect mattress for his guests. When he couldn't find exactly what he was looking for, Tony decided to design and fabricate his own exclusive mattresses for the hotel, which he made from two layers of hypoallergenic latex with a wool overlay. The carpets are imported from the Middle East and India, the wood for the furniture comes from California, Tasmania, and New Zealand, and the insulated windows – soundproofing against the roars of the stags outside – come all the way across the globe from Germany.

The food served in the lodge's restaurant, however, is an altogether more home-grown affair. The ingredients used for the exquisite evening menu are, whenever possible, sourced from local organic growers. The olive oil comes from the lodge's own specially planted grove of 800 Tuscan olive trees, and the chef picks his fresh herbs directly from the small garden in front of the treehouses.

Looking forward to the coming evening meal (the famous Kaikoura crayfish is always on the menu), I sink onto the bed with a sigh. The softness of the eiderdown is heavenly – Tony probably had it especially flown in from some faraway land. Lying there, I don't really feel like Tarzan or, more appropriately, Jane, living among the treetops. My treehouse adventure is more about exploring the many sensual comforts the treehouse has to offer. Oh well, I'll just draw myself a long, hot bath in the touchpad Jacuzzi then....

Hapuku Lodge
Comfort with style among the trees

🔘 Situated between a mountain range and the sea, around 600 ft (200 m) from the ocean. 7.5 miles (12 km) north of Kaikoura, South Island, New Zealand.

ℹ️ Five treehouses with one or two double rooms. Treehouse rental: 215–475 USD (390–855 NZD), depending on size and season.
+64 (0)3 319 6559
www.hapukulodge.com

Things to do

Swimming with dolphins
Make sure you do not miss out on a swim with Kaikoura's dolphins. It is a magical experience to meet with these wild mammals in such close proximity. The deep ocean canyon just off the coast of Kaikoura provides an abundance of food for many sea creatures, including whales, seals, and dolphins. Dusky dolphins, also called the "acrobats of the ocean" for their incredible leaps and somersaults, come close to the shore here. There's no guarantee that you will see them, and swimming is not allowed when the dolphins are accompanied by their calves. Between October and May however, it is not uncommon for a boat to encounter pods of several hundreds of dolphins – a really memorable sight.

It's a unique feeling swimming among the wild animals. Once in the water, you have to attract the dolphins' attention – after all, that's what this is about: an entertainment show for the dolphins and not the other way round! It's best to move about in a "dolphin-like" fashion as much as you can: diving down, swimming in circles, and making funny noises through your snorkel. Even if the dolphins don't find this amusing, those left on board the boat certainly will! It is truly an unforgettable experience when the curious mammals finally come close to check you out and look you straight in the eye. The dolphins really seem to want to make contact, and, in a playful kind of way, circle the snorkelers faster and faster, as though in a kind of contest, which, of course, they always win! This is an absolute must for all nature lovers.

Dolphin Encounter in Kaikoura is around 7.5 miles (12 km) from Hapuku Lodge. Tours 3 times daily in summer, 2 times daily in winter. 3–3.5-hr swim, including wet suit and snorkel: 85 USD (150 NZD).
+64 (0)3 319 6777, or toll-free in New Zealand: 0800 733 365
www.dolphin.co.nz

Trees for tourists
If you want to do more for the trees than just live among them, in Kaikoura you can have a tree planted. For 11 or 22 USD (20 or 40 NZD), you can become the owner of a native species sapling, which will grow on an idyllic hill above the town. This "eco" project aims to offset the damage of carbon emissions produced by air travel, allowing you to make a (tiny) contribution to reducing the impact of climate change.

Your very own tree will be marked, GPS-located, and from then on carefully nurtured. You can check on your tree's progress and view a regularly updated photo on the website. Or you might like to return to Kaikoura and visit your tree years later, perhaps with your grandchildren. Since some of the species will live for up to 800 years this is a lifelong natural memento of New Zealand.
+64 (0)3 319 7148
www.treesfortravellers.co.nz

Kaikoura night sky tour
During this fascinating introduction to the twinkling night sky of the southern hemisphere you will discover how to recognize the Southern Cross, and learn how the Polynesians and Captain Cook used it to navigate their way to New Zealand. When the night skies are clear, the guide Hussein Burra takes a maximum of 10 participants out to the Kaikoura Peninsula and helps them identify stars through a telescope. One of the larger planets, Saturn or Jupiter, should be clearly visible, depending on the time of year. Many use the opportunity to take a close-up photograph of the moon and its craters through the lens of the telescope.

1.5-hr tour: 28 USD (50 NZD). Departure around 1 hr after sunset.
+64 (0)3 319 6635
www.kaikouranightsky.co.nz

Above (left to right): snorkelers swimming among a pod of dolphins; Dusky dolphins; planting a sapling; taking a closer look at the night sky of the southern hemisphere

Acknowledgments

The publisher would like to thank the following for their contributions and help (in alphabetical order): Stefanie Franz (factchecking), Helen Townsend (US editor), Debra Wolter (proofreader).

Picture Credits

The publisher would like to thank the following for their kind permission to reproduce their photographs:

(Key: a-above; b-below/bottom; c-center; l-left; r-right; t-top)

Alamy Images: David Sutherland 189tr; arena Berlin: M. Mettel-Siefen 128tr, 129tl; Berlin on Bike: 128tl; Callendar House: 101tl; Camera Obscura & World of Illusions: 100tr; Conrad Maldives Rangali Island: 208, 210tr, 214tl; Dampfbahn Furka: 179tc; Destination Waitomo: 231tc; DK Images: Tony Souter 31tr; Gerard van Vuuren 118tl; Getty Images: Frank Lukasseck 21tl; Nativestock.com/Marilyn Angel Wynn 20tr; Healesville Sanctuary: 223tc; Hunter Hotels/ Gorah Elephant Camp: Nicola Schwim 198–199; Ice Hotel: 66cl; The Integratron: 36tl; Kaikoura Night Sky: Hussein Burra 239tr; Kolarbyn: Skogens Konung 73cr, 75tr; Roine Magnusson 75tl; Jenny Persson 74cl; Lion Sands Private Game Reserve: 197tc; Photolibrary: Britain on View/Natalie Pecht 93tl, 101tr; Spellbound Glowworm & Cave Tour New Zealand: 231tl; Turus Mara: Iain Morrison 93tr; Wasserwelten Göschenen: 179tr; Weg der Schweiz: 171tl; www.visitberlin.de: 129tr; Yunak Evleri: 188cl.

Jacket images: Front: Lion Sands Private Game Reserve: tl; Photolibrary: Age Fotostock/Gonzalo Azumendi bl. Back: Getty Images: Johner Images bc.

Works of art have been reproduced with the permission of the following copyright holders: Courtesy of the Noah Purifoy Foundation 38–39.

All other images © Bettina Kowalewski

10% Discount Offer

Bed in a Tree and other amazing hotels from around the world offers readers a 10% discount at the following hotels:

Dog Bark Park Inn *(see* In the Doghouse *pp14–21)*; Earthship World Headquarters *(see* Earthships *pp22–31)*; Igloo Village Kakslauttanen *(see* Glass Igloos *pp50–57)*; Kolarbyn *(see* Wood Collier's Hut *pp68–75)*; Glengorm Castle *(see* Castle *pp84–93)*; Zum Prellbock "Kofftel" *(see* Inside a Suitcase *pp130–37)*; Hotel Lindenwirt *(see* Wine Barrel *pp146–153)*; Les Roulottes *(see* Circus Wagon *pp154–63)*; La Claustra *(see* Hotel in a Mountain *pp172–9)*; Yunak Evleri *(see* Cave Hotel *pp180–87)*; Lion Sands – Chalkley and Jackalberry Treehouses *(see* Bed in a Tree *pp190–97)*; Gorah Elephant Camp *(see* Elephant Tent *pp198–205)*; Mira Mira *(see* Throat of a Troll *pp216–223)*; Woodlyn Park *(see* In a Plane *pp224–31)*; Hapuku Lodge *(see* Treehouses *pp232–9)*.

To claim your 10% discount quote "Bed in a Tree" when reserving. Valid for one reservation only. Voucher must be presented on arrival at the hotel for the discount to be fully validated. Offer expires April 30, 2011. See below for full Terms and Conditions.

Terms and Conditions

1. This promotion is open to UK, US, Canada, South Africa, Australia, and New Zealand residents aged 18 years or over, with the exception of employees of the Promoter, their families, agents, and anyone else connected with this promotion. 2. Offer valid for hotel reservations made between October 1, 2009 and April 30, 2011 for stays between the same dates. ("Promotional Period"). 3. Only one voucher per reservation. 4. Offer entitles 10% discount off the full standard rate of a standard double, twin, or single room*. Check individual hotels for availability. 5. To claim your 10% discount off the full standard rate at a participating hotel *(see list above)*, quote the reference, "Bed in a Tree," when you reserve your hotel via telephone or email. You must present your voucher to the hotel on arrival to fully validate the discount. 6. The 10% discount is deducted from the hotel's full rate. Rates quoted are per room per night based on either two people sharing a twin or double room or one person reserving a single room. Room rates may vary in price depending on the day of the week, season, and grade of room reserved. 7. Offer is only valid for advanced reservations made at the participating hotels during the Promotional Period. 8. Offer cannot be used in conjunction with any other offer and may not be available at participating hotels on certain dates. This may include named holiday periods, public holidays, and specific dates excluded by a participating hotel. Check with hotels for more information. 9. Offer subject to availability. Discounts are not redeemable for cash for any reason. 10. Photocopies, counterfeits, other reproductions, or defaced vouchers will be deemed invalid. 11. Promoter accepts no responsibility for any vouchers that are lost or damaged. 12. Promoter and the participating hotels reserve the right to vary, amend, or withdraw the offer at any time at its sole discretion. No correspondence will be entered into. 13. Promoter is responsible for the provision of vouchers. All other facilities connected with this promotion are contributed by, and are the responsibility of, the participating hotels. 14. By entering this promotion, each entrant agrees to be bound by these terms and conditions and any further terms and conditions that the participating hotels may apply at the time of booking. Promoter is Dorling Kindersley Limited of 80 Strand, London WC2R 0RL, UK.

*Except for Lion Sands where the offer entitles 10% discount off the full standard rate of the Chalkley and Jackalberry Treehouses. The offer does not apply to other accommodations at Lion Sands.

Bed in a Tree
10% off*

Chalkley and Jackalberry
Treehouses – Lion Sands
Sabi Sand Reserve
South Africa
+27 (0)11 484 9911
www.lionsands.com

OFFER ENDS 30TH APRIL 2011

Circus Wagon
10% off*

Les Roulottes – La Serve
69860 Ouroux
Rhône-Alps
France
+33 (0)4 7404 7640
www.lesroulottes.com

OFFER ENDS 30TH APRIL 2011

In a Plane
10% off*

The Plane Motel
– Woodlyn Park
Waitomo
New Zealand
+64 (0)7 878 6666
www.woodlynpark.co.nz

OFFER ENDS 30TH APRIL 2011

Treehouses
10% off*

Hapuku Lodge
Kaikoura
New Zealand
+64 (0)3 319 6559
www.hapukulodge.com

OFFER ENDS 30TH APRIL 2011

Wood Colliers' Hut
10% off*

Kolarbyn
Sweden
+46 (0)70 400 7053
www.kolarbyn.se

OFFER ENDS 30TH APRIL 2011

Elephant Tent
10% off*

Gorah Elephant Camp
Addo National Park
South Africa
+27 (0)44 501 1111
www.hunterhotels.com

OFFER ENDS 30TH APRIL 2011

Inside a Suitcase
10% off*

Zum Prellbock "Kofftel"
Saxony
Germany
+49 (0)37 383 6410
www.prellbock-bahnart.de

OFFER ENDS 30TH APRIL 2011

Cave Hotel
10% off*

Yunak Evleri
Cappadocia
Turkey
+90 (0)384 341 6920
www.yunak.com

OFFER ENDS 30TH APRIL 2011

In the Doghouse
10% off*

Dog Bark Park Inn
Idaho
USA
+1 208 962 3647
www.dogbarkparkinn.com

OFFER ENDS 30TH APRIL 2011

Throat of a Troll
10% off*

The Cave House – Mira Mira
Victoria
Australia
+61 (0)3 5626 72000
www.miramira.com.au

OFFER ENDS 30TH APRIL 2011

Castle
10% off*

Glengorm Castle
Isle of Mull
Scotland
+44 (0)1688 302 321
www.glengormcastle.co.uk

OFFER ENDS 30TH APRIL 2011

Glass Igloos
10% off*

Igloo Village
Kakslauttanen
Finland
+358 (0)16 667 100
www.kakslauttanen.fi

OFFER ENDS 30TH APRIL 2011

Hotel in a Mountain
10% off*

La Claustra
St Gotthard
Switzerland
+41 (0)91 880 5055
www.claustra.ch

OFFER ENDS 30TH APRIL 2011

Wine Barrel
10% off*

Hotel Lindenwirt
Rüdesheim-am-Rhein
Germany
+49 (0)6 722 9130
www.lindenwirt.com

Earthships
10% off*

Earthship World Headquarters
Taos
New Mexico
USA
+1 525 751 0462
www.earthship.org

OFFER ENDS 30TH APRIL 2011

BED IN A TREE
WORLD MAP

EUROPE

Glass Igloos

Ice Hotel

Wood Collier's Hut

House on a Lake

SWEDEN

FINLAND

NORWAY

DENMARK

ESTONIA

LATVIA

LITHUANIA

RUSSIAN FEDERATION

Castle

Pineapple

UNITED KINGDOM

IRELAND

Gothic Temple

NETHERLANDS

POLAND

BELARUS

Escape Capsule

Under the Stars

In a Piece of Art

Wine Barrel

Inside a Suitcase

GERMANY

CZECH REP.

UKRAINE

Prison Cell

SWITZ.

HUNGARY

Hotel in a Mountain

FRANCE

Circus Wagon

ROMANIA

ITALY

BULGARIA

SPAIN

GREECE

TURKEY

Cave Hotel

Ball in a Tree

NORTH AMERICA

Pacific Ocean

In the Doghouse

UFO

Earthships

In a Seashe

Pacific Ocean